The Bride
the Covenant, the Price, the Cup

The Perfect Love Story

Caren Apple

First published by Caren Apple, 2024
Copyright © Caren Apple, 2024

All rights reserved. No part of this publication may be reproduced, stored or transmitted in any form or by any means, electronic, mechanical, photocopying, recording, scanning, or otherwise without written permission from the publisher. It is illegal to copy this book, post it to a website, or distribute it by any other means without permission.

Unless otherwise noted, all scripture quotations are taken from the NEW KING JAMES VERSION®. Copyright© 1982 by Thomas Nelson, Inc. Used by permission. All rights reserved.

ISBN 979-8-9905587-1-7

For permission contact:
www.bocencounter.org
bocencounter@gmail.com

Cover Design By: Sue Morissey & Leo DelaCruz
Second Edition

Table of Contents

Acknowledgements
A Note from the Author
An Introduction

> The Bride of Christ
>
> The Shadchan - *The Matchmaker*
>
> The Ketubah - *Marriage Covenant*
>   i. The Mohar (*Price*)
>   ii. The Provision (*Terms*)
>   iii. Her Protection (*Conditions*)
>
> The Sefel - *Cup*
>
> The Mattanah - *Gifts*
>
> The Kallah - *Bride*
>   Mikvah - *Baptism*
>   Her Conduct During His Absence
>   Her Veil
>
> The Chupah - *The Bridal Chamber*
>
> A Tale of Imaginable Love
>
> The Chatan - *Bridegroom*
>
> A Personal Letter From Your Bridegroom
>
> Love Notes

Note: Each chapter is a fusion of an ancient Jewish traditional betrothal told within the bookmarks (📖). Though archaic, this same tradition is found in the pages of our New Testament. As we journey through time, we will begin to see and fully comprehend a Bridegrooms timeless love; without boundaries and without end, spoken in His own words (John 1:1,2).

Appendix

A Nation is Born - Israel

A Marriage Covenant of Laws - Broken

More About Our Shadchan

More About The Cup

More About The Mikvah

The Veil

The Shofar

Scripture References
Reference Study Materials
Additional Information to Consider
About the Author
Bride of Christ Encounter

Acknowledgements

Dave Apple- You have always been and forever will be the love of my life. Thank you for believing in me and never allowing me to give up on myself. I love you beyond words.

Pastor Scott Johnson- You've helped raise me to be the person I am today, and it is my hope that I will always live my life in such a way that you will be proud.

Angie Anderson- Thank you for your constant encouragement to write my vision out and for partnering with me in creating the Bride of Christ Encounter.

Ileana Harrell– Who always believed God concerning me.

Carina Fortin, Mabel Baldes, and Tina Musto: you have been my support system and I covet our deep friendship.

Sue Morrisey & Leo De La Cruz LLC – Thank you so much for helping me create my book cover.

Danielle Seykoski – You know what you did! Thank you!!

Simply Owl Design (Anna Boulier) – Thank you for your help in pushing this book through its final stages.

There are so many others who have helped to push this book to the end, and I am so thankful for every one of you.

A Note from the Author

In 2016, I picked up a booklet, written by Zola Levitts called, "A Christian Love Story". Immediately, my spirit was leaping with excitement as I began to discover familiarities between this love story and the life, and sayings of Jesus recorded in the four gospels.

The more I dug into this ancient Jewish tradition of how a young man would go to such great lengths to obtain a bride, the more I realized how precise Jesus is in following this same Jewish tradition in pursuing us as His bride.

Though this book is not an exhaustive study, my hope is to help bring revelation of a Father's absolute love, and how He had set in motion from the beginning of time to receive us as His own children and in doing so, would require Him to sacrifice His beloved Son.

"For He did not spare His own Son, but delivered Him (Jesus) up for us all, how shall He (Jesus) not with Him also freely give us all *things?*"
-Romans 8:32

An Introduction

To fully comprehend the writings of the New Testament is to understand that though Jesus was the only begotten Son of God, He also came to us as the Son of Man, in human form, and in the culture of Judaism. He lived, taught, and ministered throughout His life through a Jewish lifestyle.

Therefore, the more we are willing to learn about Jewish traditions, customs, and mannerisms, the more of an in-depth understanding we will have in the revelation and knowledge of Him; that being a bride of Christ has nothing to do with gender and has every-thing to do with position.

If you are willing to take a journey with me, I promise that you will discover, veiled in the pages of His Word, a beloved Bridegroom that is waiting for you. Allow me to share a story with you of an ancient tradition steeped in Jewish culture. It's about how a young Jewish man would go to such great lengths to pursue and win the heart of the woman he loves. Whereby, Jesus parallels this same tradition of betrothment in pursuing you as His own bride.

You were created out of a love that is absolute and

knows no boundaries. Before the foundation of the world was ever spoken into existence, you were known.

Jesus said-

"…..I have come that they may have life, and that they may have *it* <u>more abundantly</u>."

-John10:10b

His desire is to be more than your Savior, your Lord, and your King. He longs for more than a mere relationship that ties you together by His blood. He craves fellowship that reaches beyond your prayers and worship; an intimacy that can only be experienced as a bride.

Let His words capture your heart and allow His Holy Spirit to reveal to you the love of a Father who has loved you beyond all creation. Let Him love you with all the fullness of Himself; for you are His true love, His greatest gift, the love of His life, and the sole reason for His sacrifice.

Turn the page; <u>taste</u> (*experience*) and see that He is good (Ps. 34:8).

But as it is written:

"Eye has not seen, nor ear heard, nor have entered into the heart of man the things which God has prepared for those who love Him."

-1 Corinthians 2:9 (*ref. Isaiah 64:4*)

The Bride of Christ

A Jewish **Ketubah** (*marriage covenant*) was, and still considered today, a legal binding contract that was not to be thrown together haphazardly. Careful considerations had to be made in order to forge a solid Covenant bond between the **kallah** (*bride*) and the **chatan** (*bridegroom*).

It is interesting to note that the word "kallah" can be used for either a bride or daughter-in-law. It is an archaic Hebrew word that can mean both "a wasting away" or "brought to completion".

This word denotes a beautiful picture of a bride with uplifted hands extending toward her bridegroom, presenting herself as an empty vessel waiting to be filled with his hopes and dreams for a future together.

By lifting our hands in worship, we are essentially taking the position of a kallah. We do this without even realizing it because it becomes as natural to us as breathing.

As the bride of Christ, we ought to be so willing as to put aside our own hopes and dreams, desiring only to be filled with the knowledge of His will in all wisdom and spiritual understanding; that we may walk worthy of our Bridegroom, fully pleasing Him, and being fruitful in every good work (Col. 1:9,10). For God sent His only begotten Son into the world, that we might live through Him (1 John 4:9).

When we lift our hands in worship, we take the position of His kallah who is saying to their Bridegroom, "more of You Lord and less of me."

As the Apostle Paul so eloquently wrote-

> "and He died for all, that those who live <u>should live no longer for themselves</u>, but for Him who died for them and rose again."

> "Therefore, if anyone is in Christ, [they are] a new creation; <u>old things have passed away</u>, behold all things have become new."
>
> -2 Corinthians 5:15,17

And again, he says-

> "I <u>beseech</u> (*urge*) you therefore, <u>brethren</u> (*fellow believer*), by the mercies of God, that <u>you present your bodies a living sacrifice, holy, acceptable to God</u> *which is* your reasonable service.
>
> And do not be conformed to this world, but be transformed by the renewing of your mind, that you may prove *what is* that good and acceptable and perfect will of God."

-Romans 12:1,2

As His bride, the more we live our lives for our Bridegroom, the more we find that those things which held so much value and were once so important to us, appear not as much anymore. For us, to truly live is Christ, and to die is gain (Phil. 1:21).

John the Baptist said it best, "He must <u>increase</u>, but I *must* <u>decrease</u>" (John 3:30). John was saying to his disciples that he was willing to decrease by laying down his ministry and reputation in order for Jesus to achieve the highest position in the lives of others.

Therefore, we too should live our lives in such a way that it brings glory to Him. For it is in Him that we live, and move, and have our being (Acts 17:28).

Remember....

> "...you are a chosen generation, a royal priesthood, a holy nation, <u>His own special people</u>, that you may proclaim the praises of Him who called you out of darkness into His marvelous light;
>
> who once were not a people but are now the people of God, who had not obtained mercy but now have obtained mercy."
>
> -1 Peter 2:9,10

"For God so loved the world that <u>He gave His only begotten Son,</u> that whoever believes in Him should not perish but have everlasting life."

- John 3:16

The Shadchan

The Matchmaker

📖 The lives of the Jewish people were very simple, and for that reason there was no room for courting or dating. Marriage was a legality, merely a business transaction between the prospective bridegroom and the father of the bride.

Young men were strongly encouraged to marry between the ages of 18-20, and girls were given permission to marry as early as twelve years old. Now I know what you are thinking, *"she is WAY too young,"* but we must understand that the Jewish culture, even before the time of Jesus, was very different than it is today. Children, as soon as they were able, were expected to work and contribute to the family.

A young girl at that age was fully capable of managing a household: washing clothes, making bread, fetching water, planning the family meals, sewing her own clothes, taking care of smaller siblings, and working in the fields if needed. Even at that age, she would be capable of going to the marketplace by herself to buy, sell, and barter for goods.

She literally would be, in the sense of today, considered a responsible adult woman capable of holding down a job, paying bills, driving a car, as well as fully managing and raising a family. It is easy to see how invaluable she was and what a great loss it would be to her family if she was to leave.

When the parents of a young man felt that their son was ready for marriage, they would seek out a **shadchan** (a *matchmaker*). This was not uncommon and is still used, to some extent, in modern Jewish communities today.

The reputation of the shadchan rested solely on their ability to find a compatible match and to arrange a contractual agreement of marriage. Their services were not to acquire a reasonable price for a bride, but rather to find the perfect bride, no matter the cost.

Therefore, these matches were not put together spontaneously or by chance. It was the business of the shadchan to get to know everyone in the community as well as the outskirts of town to find that perfect match. You could say that they were the town's busybodies who made it a priority to be involved in everyone's business. After all, that is how they made their living.

When a prospective match was found, the shadchan would approach the potential bride's father, on behalf of the family they were representing, with an offer of marriage. If the father was interested, he would agree to enter into a mediation period that would determine the price, terms, and conditions of her Ketubah; a Marriage

Covenant written solely on his daughter's behalf.

Once mediation was initiated, the shadchan would then transition from a matchmaker to the position of a mediator; a type of marriage broker who equally represented both parties. The time it took for these contractual proceedings to finalize could take, quite possibly, up to several months. Just the bride price (*mohar*) alone could take weeks of endless negotiations and persistent haggling before a final agreement between the two parties was achieved; and having an experienced shadchan representing both sides was vital to the mediation process.

When the match had been brokered and the bride's price determined, the Ketubah would then be drawn up by the bridegroom's father and witnessed by the shadchan. The Ketubah would then be handed to the son who would take it to the potential bride's home and officially present it to her father.

If the father was not living, the Ketubah would be handed over to the oldest living male relative, as was the case with Rebekah and Isaac in Geneses 24. 📖

As we read our own **Ketubah** (*New Testament*) through the spiritual eyes of a betrothed bride, we begin to see so patently how God, from the beginning of time, had set Himself up as the **Shadchan**, both to Jews and Gentiles. And in doing so, has set in motion a covenant bond between His beloved Son and all the inhabitants of the world who would receive Him.

> "But God, who is rich in mercy, because of His great love with which He loved us,

> even when we were dead in <u>trespasses</u> (*our sins*), made us alive together with Christ (by grace you have been saved)
>
> and <u>raised *us* up together</u> [with Him], and <u>made *us* sit together</u> [with Him} in the heavenly *places* in Christ Jesus,"
>
> -Ephesians 2:4-6

God took one man, a Gentile from his native land Ur, and birthed a nation. And it is through this nation, Israel, that our Savior Jesus came. In Him pertains our everlasting Marriage Covenant, and it is in Him to which the eternal promises of God extend to all who believe in His Son.

> "In past generations it was not made known to mankind, as the Spirit is now revealing it to His <u>emissaries</u> (*apostles*) and prophets; that in union with the Messiah and through the Good News the Gentiles were to be joint heirs, a joint body, and joint shares with the Jews in what God had promised."
> -Ephesians 3:5,6 (Complete Jewish Bible)

Think about this- God, the Creator of the UNIVERSE, negotiated the terms and price of our betrothment to His beloved Son simply because He loves us with an everlasting love that knows no boundaries!

Our invitation to receive Jesus, though it was of our own free will, did not occur by happenstance. We were individually <u>chosen</u> as a perfect match for His Son.

> "just as He (*God*) <u>chose us</u> in Him (*Jesus*) before the foundation of the world, that we should be

holy and without blame before Him in love."
-Ephesians 1:4

The ability to believe, in and of itself, is a gift from God!

> "for you have been delivered by grace through trusting [Him], and even this is not your accomplishment but God's gift."
> -Ephesians 2:8 (CJB)

In fact, there is one scripture that we have read and heard so many times before that we, most likely, have become impervious to it over time.

> "For God so loved the world that **He gave** His only begotten Son, that whoever believes in Him should not perish but have everlasting life."
> -John 3:16

I believe Christians today have used John 3:16 more than any other verse as a witness and testimony. However, did you know that this single verse holds a mystery hidden in plain sight?

If you did not know about the historic background to a Jewish betrothment, and how Jesus parallels this same tradition step by step in pursuing us today, you would pass this verse by time and time again, not even realizing that it is the catalyst to our very salvation!

Read John 3:16 once more, this time with a new understanding, that can only be seen through the eyes of a bride.

> For God so loved the world (*the people*) that **He gave** [in betrothment] His only born Son, that whoever believes in Him should not perish but

have everlasting life [in His Kingdom].

It took God, our **Shadchan**, several thousand years to align everything into perfect position before He would present His offer of marriage, on behalf of His beloved Son, to the world.

God's perfect love set in motion a strategic plan that would bring both Jews and Gentiles together in one body, through the cross; a love that would require Him to sacrifice His own beloved Son that we may have eternal life with Him.

> "... that He (*Jesus*) might reconcile them both (*Jews and Gentiles*) to God in one body through the cross, thereby putting to death the enmity.
>
> And He came and preached peace to you [Gentiles] who were afar off and to those [Jews] who were near.
>
> For through Him we both have access by one Spirit to the Father.
>
> -Ephesians 2 16-18

And it is only the brides of Christ who can truly know that the Son of God *has* come!

> "And we know that the Son of God has come and has given us an understanding, that we may know Him who is true; and we are in Him who is true, in His Son Jesus Christ. This is the true God and eternal life."
>
> -1 John 5:20

This is where we are! Seriously, how cool is that!

"...The kingdom of heaven is like a merchant seeking beautiful pearls, who, when he found one pearl of great price, went and sold all that he had and bought it."

-Matthew 13:45,46

The Ketubah

Marriage Covenant

📖 Upon receiving the **Ketubah**, the father would read it aloud before the entire family as a witness. In it contained three essential key components: price, terms and conditions, with each element explicitly written on the prospective bride's behalf.

i. The **mohar** (*bride price*), which was given to the father, was expected to be a substantial amount, as the payment would be a type of recompense and compensation for the loss of labor due to her leaving the household. It was also meant to show the expression of his love. Anything less than his best would be insulting.

(In farming & agricultural communities, a father with a family of sons was considered more profitable because of the gained workforce, whereas daughters were considered more of a liability since she was expected to leave the family when she became old enough to marry).

ii. It ascribed, in precise detail, **terms** that were required to be carried out. These terms were assurances that she would be provided for financially and be given a safe and secure environment so long as she lived.

iii. There would be certain **conditions** put in place to protect her should he decide to put her aside during the betrothal period or in the event of his death. In which case, the mohar would then be forfeited to her family and she would be entitled to keep any gifts given to her by the bridegroom: land, livestock, money, jewelry, etc.

It also ascribed certain safeguards should he decide to divorce her, or renege on any part of the contract during their marriage. In modern terms, you could consider the Ketubah a type of prenuptial agreement that was made solely on her behalf as a means of protection. 📖

Now, if Jesus, our bridegroom, did indeed follow this same ancient Jewish tradition, then He too would be obligated to uphold these same contractual agreements.

Let's see if He does-

i. **The Mohar**- Let me begin by asking you this...

What is the value of a life?
Would you hesitate to kill a bug crawling on your wall or swat a fly that was threatening to land on your food?

Would you not at once call the exterminator to schedule an appointment that would eradicate all unwanted pests and rodents in and around your home?

Or would you just gently pick up a cockroach crawling across your floor and walk it to the door hoping it doesn't return? I doubt that anyone would place the smallest value on the life of an unwanted pest. Although, in all fairness, I once saw my brother capture a carpenter ant and put it outside.

The answer to my question is simply this: "Life only has value in the eyes of the beholder."

What about your life?

What is the value of <u>your</u> life?

Jesus says-

> ...."I have come that you may have life, and that you may have it more abundantly."
>
> -John 10:10b

However, this amazing life that we live in Christ could only have come by way of an incomparable, undefiled, and incorruptible **mohar** price.

Jesus says-

> "Just as the Son of Man did not come to be served, but to serve, and to <u>give</u> His life [as] a <u>ransom</u> for many [YOU]."
>
> -Matthew 20:28

The word, "give" in Matthew 20:28 (1325 Louw and Nida Greek-English Lexicon of the New Testament) literally means, "*to give one's life*" and "*to die willingly*". It can also be translated as, "*to permit oneself to be killed*" or "*to allow others to kill oneself.*"

Also, the word "ransom" in this verse, comes from the Greek word, "lutron" (3083, 3084 Strong's Greek/Hebrew Definitions) which means, *"something to loose with"* i.e. *a redemption price.*

Interestingly, Paul tells us in his letter to Titus, that Jesus gave Himself for us that <u>He might redeem</u> us from every lawless deed and purify for Himself His own special people, zealous for good works (Titus 2:14). The words, "He might redeem" likewise come from the Greek word *"lutron."*

However, it was not His body that loosened us from the shackles of sin. It was something that He carried with Him from the time of His birth, far more precious than anything that could be made with human hands.

> "knowing that you were not <u>redeemed</u> (*bought*) with <u>corruptible</u> (*perishable*) things, *like* silver or gold, from your aimless conduct received by tradition from <u>your fathers</u> (*generations past*),
>
> but **with the precious blood of Christ**, as of a lamb without blemish and without spot."
> -1 Peter 1:18,19

Paul says-

> [It is] "In Him [that] we have redemption **through His blood**, the forgiveness of sins, according to the riches of His grace"
> -Ephesians 1:7

Jesus' **mohar** that He so willing paid, was His priceless blood, sacrificed on God's altar, the cross! I encourage you to read Ephesians, Chapter 2 in its entirety.

> "But now in Christ Jesus you who once were far off have been **brought near by the blood** of Christ."
>
> -Ephesians 2:13

Also-

> "and that He might reconcile them both (*Jews and Gentiles*) to God in one body through the cross, thereby putting to death the enmity.
>
> -Ephesians 2:16

It is the redemptive price of His blood that we receive forgiveness of sins, and it is by His sacrificed life that we obtain eternal life.

I love what Paul says-

> "For I am persuaded that neither death nor life, nor angels nor principalities, nor powers, nor things present nor things to come,
>
> nor height nor depth, nor any other created thing, shall be able to separate *(put space between us)* from the love of God which is in Christ Jesus our Lord."
>
> -Romans 8:38,39

The manifestation of God's love towards us is unfathomable and cannot be expressed with just mere words. But Paul certainly tries with this verse.

> "But God demonstrates (*proves the existence of*) His own love toward us, in that while we were still

sinners (unbelievers), Christ died for us.

Much more then, having now been **justified** (*saved*) **by His blood**, we shall be saved from wrath through Him."

-Romans 5:8,9

Hebrews 12:2 tells us that He is the author and the finisher, the originator and the perfecter of our faith, who for the joy- of seeing you with Him- endured the cross, despising the shame, and is now seated at the right-hand side of God. It was finished, it is finished, and it will forever be finished, Amen!!

He made this decision concerning you in full obedience to the Father, without partiality, and without hesitation!

ii. **The Terms –**

If you have a Bible that carries the New Testament, you have a Ketubah, a Marriage Covenant written specifically on your behalf. In it carries all the promises of provision that are guaranteed to you during your stay here as His betrothed bride.

Paul tells us in his second letter to Timothy (3:16) that all scriptures are given by the inspiration of God, meaning that every word spoken from the pages of your Ketubah is literally "*God breathed.*" And it is to your own benefit for you to know what is written.

Peter shares with us from his own experiences with Jesus-

> "as His divine power has given to us all things that *pertain* to life and godliness, through the

> knowledge of Him (*Jesus*) who called us by glory and virtue,
>
> by which have been given to us exceedingly great and precious promises, that through these [the promises] you may be partakers of [His] divine nature, having escaped the corruption that is in the world through [the world's] lust."
>
> -2 Peter 1:3,4

It is by His divine power that we have all things needed to carry out an abundant life and to walk a life of godliness. Jesus tells us that He has come that we may have life and *that* life gives us the power to live our lives to its fullest, in abundance, through Him (John 10:10).

> "For all the promises of God in Him (*Jesus*) *are* Yes, and in Him Amen, to the glory of God **through us**."
>
> -2 Corinthians 1:20

Every promise that comes from the spoken word of God is Yes- meaning it is for sure and for certain. And in Him Amen- simply put, that's it and that's all.

Paul says-

> "And my God will supply all your need according to His riches in glory **by** Christ Jesus."
>
> -Philippians 4:19

iii. The Conditions- put in place to protect her should he decide to put her aside (divorce or change his mind during the betrothment).

There has always been an argument as to whether we

could lose our salvation. You could almost justify the possibility of that happening just by reading the third key element in this legal document.

However, God Himself has added an amendment to our Ketubah that strikes this third element from ever happening. That Amendment is called –

"ADOPTION".

Did you know that Jesus refers to God as Father more than by any other name? Over 250 times! The New Testament is full of scriptures that give no doubt to God's desire of having children to fill His kingdom.

Several times in his letters, Paul reveals God's heart towards us as a Father with the privilege we are given of calling Him, "Abba".

> "For you did not receive the spirit of bondage again to <u>fear</u> (*the fear of losing your salvation*), but you received the Spirit of adoption by whom we cry out, "**Abba, Father.**"
>
> The Spirit Himself bears witness with our spirit that **we are children of God**,"
> -Romans 8:15,16

In a Jewish home, only a child who has been born to the patriarch of that household has the privilege to call him "Abba". It is not permitted for a servant, close relative, or another child outside of the home to call the head of the household, "Abba."

However, God has given *all* who receive His beloved

Son, Jesus, the right and privilege of calling Him, "Abba," without fear.

> "And because you are sons (*this is a place of position, not gender*), God has sent forth the Spirit of His Son into your hearts, crying out, "**Abba, Father**"!
> -Galatians 4:6

This is surely a Selah moment- God does not want servants, mindless followers, or stepchildren in His kingdom. He longs, with His whole heart, children to fill His kingdom. He desires to hear our laughter, our praise, and our joy of heart.

And look what Paul says here-

> "having predestined (*determined in advance*) us to adoption as [His] children by Jesus Christ to Himself, according to the good pleasure of His will,
>
> to the praise of the glory of His grace, by which He made us accepted in the Beloved (*Jesus*)."
> -Ephesians 1:5,6

Just these few scriptures allow us to see so clearly the seriousness, determination, and full commitment of our Father's love toward His children, YOU!

Think about this- we have an amazing privilege of calling the Creator of the entire universe, "Daddy"! Seriously, can we just take a second here to pause and attempt to wrap our heads around this amazing privilege!?

And if this revelation alone does not fully convince you

that your place has been solidified by an adoption process that can NEVER be revoked, can NEVER be annulled, and will NEVER be rescinded, I've got more to show you!

> "For the Lord Himself will descend from heaven with a shout, with a voice of an archangel, and with the trumpet of God. And the <u>dead in Christ</u> (*those who have passed away*) will rise first.
>
> Then we who are alive and remain **shall be caught up** together with them in the clouds to meet the Lord in the air. And thus, we shall always be with the Lord."
> -1 Thessalonians 4:16,17 (*see also* Mark 13:26,27)

The words "shall be caught up" is one word and it is the Greek word, "*harpazo*" (726 Strong Concordance) and it can mean- "*to catch away, to be plucked, or to take by force.*" Incidentally, this same Greek word "*harpazo,*" in Latin, is "*rapturo,*" where we get our English word "*rapture.*" This is very significant, and it will come together in the next verse.

Jesus says-

> "My <u>sheep</u> (*true believers*) hear My voice, and I know them, and they follow Me.
>
> <u>And I give them eternal life</u>, and <u>they shall never perish</u>; neither shall anyone **snatch** them out of My hand.
>
> My Father, who has given *them* to Me, is greater than all; and no one is able to **snatch** *them* out of My Father's hand.

> I and My Father are one."
>
> - John 10:27-30

This word "snatch" is also the Greek word, "*harpazo*" which means- the same exact force that will one day remove us from this planet is the very same exact force that holds us in the very palm of our Fathers hand!

Did you happen to catch the other two statements He made- "And I give them eternal life," AND "they shall never perish" Jesus is saying that the life that we now live is perpetual, never ending, and timeless. We shall NEVER grow old, be destroyed, or experience death. So, let me ask you this, are you a sheep- I know I am!

Jesus says-

> "At that day (*Rev. 1:7*) you will know that I *am* in My Father, and you in Me, and I in you."
>
> -John 14:20

We are so intertwined with God; it is impossible for us to be released from the grasp of the love that holds us in Him. Not only is it important that we know who we are and to whom we belong, but it is just as crucial to know exactly WHERE we are "*in Him*". And don't even get me started on those verses.

One day our Bridegroom will come and those of us who are blessed to see His arrival on this side of heaven will experience the most glorious promise coming to fruition before our very eyes- the beginning of our eternal life!

And of course, I must at least mention the statement that has been known to divide churches.

"Once Saved, Always Saved"

But if you ask the question and truly understand what you are asking, the answer would be an emphatic YES!

Anyone can say the words, "I am a Christian" or "I believe in Jesus," but these are mere words. The Apostle Paul says it best with such simplicity that I find it hard to argue otherwise. And twice he quotes Old Testament scriptures.

> "that if you <u>confess</u> (*acknowledge*) with your mouth the Lord Jesus and believe in your heart that God has raised Him from the dead, you will be <u>saved</u> (*delivered, protected, preserved, healed, made whole*).
>
> For with the heart, one believes unto righteousness, and with the mouth confession is made unto salvation.
>
> For the scripture says, 'Whoever believes on Him will not be put to shame.'
>
> For there is no distinction between Jew and Greek (*Gentiles*). For the same Lord over all is rich to all who call upon Him.
>
> For '**whoever calls** [and believes] **on the name of the Lord shall be saved**."
> -Romans 10:9-13 (Joel 2:32)

Paul also says-

> "even the righteousness of God, <u>through faith in Jesus Christ</u>, to all and on all <u>who believe</u>. For

there is no difference;

for all have sinned and fall short of the glory of God.,

> Being justified (*saved*) freely by His grace through the redemption that is in Christ Jesus."
> -Romans 3:22-24

Don't let yourself be trapped in the legalism of your salvation, let alone anyone else's. God forbid if we become brave enough to judge another.

Ok, back to the Story-

📖 It might surprise you that neither the young man nor the potential bride was involved in any decision making concerning the Ketubah or the match itself.

The son may have known ahead of time what was written out, but he certainly did not have a say as to what would be negotiated between families. He was simply expected to obey his father. 📖

I can't help but to interject here- this made me think about what Paul said concerning our Bridegroom-

> "And being found in appearance as a man, He humbled Himself and <u>became obedient</u> to the point of death, even death of the cross."
> -Philippians 2:8

Our Bridegroom knew full well of His Father's plan in how He would redeem us back to Himself. John 1:1,2 tells us that He was fully involved in the writings of our

Ketubah.

📖 You would also think at this point that we would have heard something about the bride and her thoughts on the matter- I assure you, she does have a say. She has the right to accept or refuse the offer of marriage. If she did not agree or wasn't interested in the one calling upon her, she could simply say no but then she risked not ever being approached again with another offer.

There also was a slight possibility that she would be pressured to marry. Some reasons may include the bride's price being too good to pass up, or quite possibly, for the bringing together of two families for the purpose of peace.

Whatever the matter, she still had a say as to whether she wanted to marry. 📖

Can you not see your worth written in the pages of your own Ketubah? There are so many mysteries and revelations that are waiting to be discovered; hidden in plain sight. He is even willing to go over it with a fine-tooth comb with you if you are willing to press into His Holy Spirit.

Do you not see how valuable you are? Why would you receive Him with your whole heart and then live your life wondering if He really loves you? Remember, **He chose you**, you did not choose Him (John 15:16,19).

"I thirst!"

- John 19:28b

The Sefel

The Cup

📖 If she agreed, the contract would be signed by the one who would be giving her away (*her father*), and by the one who would be taking responsibility for her (*the bridegroom*). With the contract signed, they would simply share a **sefel** (*cup*) of wine together, thus legally binding them as one accord.

Now you might not think so, but the sefel was very significant to the process of becoming betrothed to one another. Drinking the contents was as equally binding as Americans today going to a County Courthouse, signing a marriage license, and having it filed. For all intents and purposes, they were legally man and wife.

Only if the contractual agreement were broken could the marriage become null and void, as was the infidelity charge against Mary- Joseph had plans to put her aside quietly and would have if the Spirit of the Lord had not interceded on her behalf - see Matthew 1:19. (*ref. to the law is found in Deut. 22:13-30, specifically v.20,21).*

The sefel represented a blood covenant between them in which they were then considered legally betrothed to one another. This is the equivalent of a minister announcing, "I now pronounce you man and wife." But be that as it may, they would not consummate their marriage or see each other for a better part of a year.

This would also be the last time that they would drink from the vine for it was traditional for both bride and bridegroom to abstain from drinking wine until they came together once again. 📖

This should sound very familiar to us for Jesus said this very same thing during His last Passover.

> "But I say to you, I will not drink of this fruit of the vine <u>from now on</u> until that day when I drink it new with you in My Father's house."
> -Matthew 26:29

Traditionally, we tend to put great importance on getting baptized as soon as we say the "Salvation" prayer. And though I would agree that there is significance in being baptized, I personally do not agree that it should be as much of a priority as I do in taking communion; knowing why we do it and the true meaning of the cup we drink from.

In the time of Acts, there certainly was justification for new believers (who were at one time being publicly baptized in the name of their false gods) to be baptized in front of witnesses straight away. Peter understood this and called upon those new believers to repent, turn against those same false gods, and be publicly baptized in the name of God the Father, God the Son, and God the Holy Spirit.

Jesus says-

> "Therefore, whoever confesses Me before <u>men</u> (*mankind*), him I will also <u>confess</u> (*acknowledge*) before My Father who is in heaven."
> -Matthew 10:32

Each time we take the sefel during communion, we take the position of a bride of Christ. Jesus tells us in Luke 22:19, **"do this in remembrance of Me."**

Whether at church, a corporate setting, or home alone, communion is meant to be a private and intimate moment between us and our beloved Bridegroom.

For it is with thanksgiving-

- We remember that at one time we were without Christ, having no hope and without God, alone in the world. But now in Him we who were once <u>afar off</u> (*unsaved*), have been brought near by the blood price of Jesus (Eph. 2:13,14).

- We remember that Christ has <u>redeemed</u> (*bought*) us from the curse of the law (for the Jews who were under it and for the Gentiles who were without it) having become a curse for us (Gal. 3:13).

- We remember how much He loved us and had given Himself for us, an offering, and a sacrifice to God for a sweet-smelling aroma (Eph. 5:2).

- We remember that our bodies are the temple of His Holy Spirit who lives in us, and we are not our own, for we were bought at an incomparable price (1 Cor. 3:16 & 6:19,20).

- We remember the cup that we take from is the new covenant in His blood. And as often as we drink from it, **we are to remember** Him and proclaim He death until He comes [for His bride] (1 Cor. 11:25,26).

There is so much to remember and be thankful for. Each time we take communion and drink from the sefel, it should always put us in remembrance of the price He so willingly paid, without reluctance, and without hesitation. By His own free will He endured the cross that He may take back what was His from the very beginning, YOU!

Oh, that Christ may dwell in our hearts through faith; that we who are being rooted and grounded in His love may be able to comprehend what is the width, and length, and depth, and height of our Bridegrooms love, and that we may be filled with all the fullness of God (Eph. 3:17-19).

Did you know it was God Himself who specifically chose you for His beloved Son?

> "Just as He (*God*) chose us in Him (*Jesus*) before the foundation of the world, that we should be holy and [seen] without blame before Him in love."
> -Ephesians 1:4

And it was Jesus' inexpressible and unimaginable perfect love that so willingly paid the price for our betrothment.

> "In Him (*Jesus*) we have redemption through His blood [payment that gave us] the forgiveness of [all] sins, according to the riches of His (*God's*) grace
> -Ephesians 1:7

There still does remain an unanswered question here-

When did Jesus receive His portion?

If Jesus was following this same tradition in His pursuit of us, then when would He have received His portion of the cup?

We know He did not receive His portion during His last Passover meal with the disciples. The cup He instructed them to divide amongst themselves was set aside specifically for them (Luke 22:17). His portion of the cup would come from another; one that we would not be able to drink from, one that His Father had set aside for Him alone.

> "So, Jesus said to Peter, "Put your sword into the sheath. Shall I not drink **the cup** which My Father has given Me?"
> -John 18:11

This incident happened in the Garden of Gethsemane, when the soldiers were attempting to arrest Him. Therefore, Jesus had not yet received His portion of the cup.

Let's trace His steps and see if He, in fact, did receive His portion which would have solidified His betrothal to us.

When the disciples met in the upper room- for what they did not know would be their last Passover meal together-

Jesus said-

> "'.....With *fervent* desire I have desired to eat this Passover with you before I suffer;
>
> for I say to you, I will no longer <u>eat of it</u> (*the Passover meal*) until it is fulfilled in the kingdom of God.'
>
> Then He took the cup, and gave thanks, and said-
>
> 'Take <u>this</u> (*the cup*) and **divide it among yourselves**; for I say to you, I will not drink of the fruit of the vine until the kingdom of God comes.'
>
> And He took bread, gave thanks and broke it, and gave it to them, saying-
>
> 'this is My body which is given for you; do this in remembrance of Me.'
>
> Likewise, He also took the cup after supper, saying-
>
> 'This is the **new covenant <u>in</u> My blood**, which is shed for you.'"

-Luke 22:15-20

The disciples were drinking from the cup that represented His blood covenant. Jesus would NOT have drunk from this cup since it represented His own blood.

When He was in the Garden of Gethsemane, He prayed twice that the cup God had prepared for Him could pass.

> "He went a little further and fell on His face, and prayed, saying, 'O My Father, if it is possible, let this cup pass from Me; nevertheless, not as I will but as You will.'"
>
> -Matthew 26:39

And -

> "'Again, a second time, He went away and prayed, saying, 'O My Father, if this cup cannot pass away from Me unless I drink it, Your will be done.'"
>
> -Matthew 26:42

This tells us clearly that Jesus still had not received His portion of the sefel (*cup*). That leaves one more place, and if you were not looking for it, you might easily miss it.

Our Bridegroom received His portion ON THE CROSS!! It is the last thing He said and did before He gave up His Spirit.

> "After this, Jesus, knowing that all things were now accomplished, that the Scriptures might be fulfilled, said, 'I thirst!'

> Now <u>a vessel</u> (*His cup*) full of sour wine was sitting there; and they filled a sponge with sour wine, put it on hyssop, and put it to His mouth.
>
> So, when Jesus had <u>received the sour wine</u>, He said, 'It is finished!' And bowing His head, He gave up His Spirit."
>
> -John 19:28-30

Before the gospel was presented to you by the One whose love towards you is limitless; before you believed and accepted His absolute love; before you were sealed with the Holy Spirit of promise; three words were uttered on the cross, "IT IS FINISHED!"

So many will try and spiritualize this last statement that Jesus made. But there is no reason why Jesus would say this other than to fulfill His position as a loving Bridegroom who paid the ultimate price to have the bride He had desired since the beginning of time, YOU!

Taking communion, in my opinion, is the most personal, intimate aspect of our relationship with our Bridegroom. A private and cherished moment that no matter how many people you are around, there are only the two of you in the room.

The **Ketubah** (_____) has been presented; the **mohar** (_____) with the bride's agreement to the Covenant promise has been accepted; and the bridegroom and bride have shared the **sefel** (_____), thus solidifying the betrothment between them. And there you have the-

Covenant, the Price, the Cup

However, there is one more item that needs to be taken care of before he departs; the **Mattanah**.

"Every good gift and every perfect gift is from above, and comes down from the Father of lights, with whom there is no variation or shadow of turning."

-James 1:17

The Mattanah

Gifts

📖 It was traditional for the bridegroom to bestow a **Mattanah** (*gifts*) upon her. These gifts were intended to take care of any needs she might have while he was away. Also, it was considered a type of guarantee on a promise made that he would return for her.

The Mattanah could be a variety of things: jewelry, money, livestock, and/or goods. If the bridegroom was well off, he could bestow upon her servants or even *land.

> *The exception to this type of gift was that she would have to be of the same tribe as her bridegroom. The inheritance of land could not change hands from tribe to tribe as was stated by law. (*ref.* Num. 36:7,8)

Isaac and Rebekah again would be a notable example to use concerning the giving of both the **Mohar**, which is the (_____), and the **Mattanah** (Gen. 24).

Abraham sent his oldest servant, Eliezer, to the family of his descendants in Mesopotamia so that he might find a bride for his son, Isaac. After seeking God on finding the perfect match, he came upon Rebekah whom he gave gifts to for watering his camels and in hopes that he could secure her as a potential bride.

Upon her family's agreement to let her marry and Rebekah's acceptance of the offer of marriage, the servant gave a bride price to her mother and Laban, her brother (the father must have passed). He then gave gifts to Rebekah: jewelry of silver and gold, and clothing.

If you travel back to Genesis 24, you will notice that Eliezer took the position of a Shadchan for Abraham *and* sought God with regard to finding the perfect match for Isaac- this would be the perfect time to interject the importance of seeking our Father for the perfect match with regard to you or a loved one. 📖

God the Father, God the Son, and God the Holy Spirit has made sure that the gifts bestowed upon us are a representation that every need will be met as they occur-

> "And my God shall supply all your need according to His riches in glory by Christ Jesus."
> -Philippians 4:19

> "......for your heavenly Father knows that you need all these things. But seek first the kingdom of God and His righteousness, and all these things [you are in need of] shall be added to you."
> -see Matthew 6:25-34 (vs. 32,33)

As well as uphold the promise of our Bridegroom's soon return-

> "For all the promises of God in Him are Yes, and in Him Amen, to the glory of God through us, [the believers].
>
> Now He who establishes us with you in Christ and has anointed us is God,
>
> who also has sealed us and <u>given us the Spirit in our hearts as a **guarantee**</u>."
> -2 Corinthians 1:20-22

Also-

> "Now He who has prepared us for this very thing *is* God, who also has <u>given us the Spirit as a **guarantee**</u>.
> -2 Corinthians 5:5

Once more-

> "In Him, [Jesus], you also *trusted*, after you heard the word of truth, the gospel of your salvation; in whom also, having believed, you were sealed with <u>the Holy Spirit of promise,</u>
>
> <u>who is the **guarantee**</u> of our inheritance until the redemption of the purchased possession to the praise of His glory."
> -Ephesians 1:13,14

The word, "guarantee," is of Hebrew origin (Old Testament, Strong's Concordance, 6162). And it is only found in these three New Testament scriptures. Vine's

Expository Dictionary of New Testament Words describes this word as, "earnest-money, deposited by the purchaser and forfeited if the purchase was not complete".

This is an amazing find to me! It reinforces solid evidence that Jesus is following the same ancient Jewish tradition in His pursuit of us, as found in the third element, (_____), mentioned in the bride's Ketubah in a previous chapter! Remember it?

Jesus did not just give you tangible gifts that fade away and deteriorate over time. He gave you Himself, His Holy Spirit, as a personal **guarantee** that He will never leave you nor would He ever forsake you. Which simply means that He has no intentions of leaving you alone nor leaving you behind (Hebrew 13:5).

You are His purchased possession; His precious blood was the mohar (_____), paid in full, and He has full intentions of coming back for His bride- YOU!

And of course, I couldn't leave this chapter without mentioning personal gifts given to us by our beloved Bridegroom.

> "But to each one of us grace was given according to the measure of Christ's gift (***Mattanah***).
>
> Therefore, He says:
>
> "When He ascended in high, He led captivity captive, and gave gifts to men (*mankind*)."
> -Ephesians 4:7,8

And-

> "... He Himself gave *some* to be apostles, *some* prophets, *some* evangelists, and *some* pastors and teachers.
>
> For the equipping of the saints for the work of the ministry, for the edifying of the body of Christ,"
> -Ephesians 4:11,12

As you can see, Paul mentions the word, "some" four times in his text. I have found that when a word is mentioned several times, it is worth finding out what they were trying to convey. It is the Greek work, "*ho*" included with the feminine word, "*he*". This Greek word (3588 Strong's Greek/Hebrew Definitions), is a neutral word that can mean, "*he, she, or one.*"

This is important, especially for some of us women, who have struggled in ministry due to some religions that believe women cannot be pastors and teachers before a congregation of both men and women.

Paul is saying here that Jesus has given the gift of Apostleship, Prophet, Evangelist, and yes, Pastors and Teachers to both men and women. The fact that Paul was repetitive in his statement leaves no room for debate. And I have to say, "I love my gift!"

📖 Last, but not least, before the bridegroom departed, he would make a promising vow to his now betrothed bride that would go something like this:

> *"I go to my father's house to make ready a place for you. I do not know when I will return, only my father knows. However, I give you a promise that I will return for you, I will not forsake coming to you. Wait for me,*

my beloved."

And with that he leaves, no kiss good-bye, no lingering hug; she will not see him again for the better part of a year, maybe longer. As he said, only his father will know when he will return for his bride.

This as well should sound very familiar to you. For this is what Jesus said to His disciples, on the night of His last Passover with the exception of one, his betrayer, Judas Iscariot. And it is very much intended for us as well.

> "Let not your heart be troubled [_____ (your name)]; you believe in God [your Father], believe also in Me [your Bridegroom]. In My Fathers house are many rooms; if it were not so, I would have told you. I go to prepare a place for you. And if I go and prepare a place for you, I will come again and receive you to Myself; that where I am, there you may be also."
>
> -John 14:1-3

Here's something also to think about- When we get engaged, we too are given a Mattanah from our fiancé, usually in the form of a ring. That ring not only symbolizes his love and devotion, but also to a promise given that when the set date arrives, he will be there to honor his commitment-.

Jesus has also made a promise that when the set date of His return is at hand, He too will be there to receive us. However, He does not know when it will be since our Father is keeping that information very close to the vest.

> "But of that day and hour, [of My return], no one

> knows, not even the angels of heaven, but My Father only."
>
> -Matthew 24:36

Why wouldn't Jesus know the moment His Father would release Him to come for His bride?! Once again, He is following the traditions of a Jewish betrothment.

(When you read the chapter on, "The Chatan" it will all come together for you! Until then, read on- don't cheat).

Just as the young bride will wait for the return of her beloved bridegroom, so too, we wait for our Beloved!

"Let us be glad and rejoice and give Him glory, for the marriage of the Lamb has come, and His wife has made herself ready. And to her it was granted to be arrayed in fine linen, clean and bright, for the fine linen is the righteousness acts of the saints."

- Revelation 19:7,8

The Kallah

The Bride

So far, we have learned how an ancient Jewish tradition of betrothment took place. Now let us take a quick look at how the bride's time will be spent during the separation period.

📖 Her bridegroom has just left her father's house, and she finds herself now legally betrothed to a man she will not see again for the better part of a year, maybe longer. Though he would be busy every moment of the day preparing for her arrival, time for her, on the other hand, would seem to move at a snail's pace.

There was very little for her to do in preparation for her wedding day: go through a ritual cleansing (*Mikvah*), choose her bridesmaids, make her own wedding gown, and, well, that's it.

Most importantly, she was to stay vigilant of his return, conduct herself in a manner that would be pleasing to him while he was away, and stay faithful no matter the cost. In short, she was expected to live her life in such a way that would bring honor to his household for she was not her own any longer; she was bought at a price.

This is where we are in the story, waiting for our beloved Bridegroom's return. However, for us, there is much to do and thousands of day-to-day decisions that need to be made concerning our own conduct and behavior; our lives are not as simple as it was in the time of Jesus.

> "<u>Watch</u> therefore, for you do not know what <u>hour</u> (*day*) your Lord is coming."
> -Matthew 24:42

Jesus, Himself, tells us to be <u>watchful</u> (1127 Strong's Greek/Hebrew Definitions); *stay awake, keep watch, be vigilant*, for we do not know when He is coming. And as the bride of Christ, we too are expected to conduct ourselves in a manner that brings glory and honor to our Bridegroom while we wait patiently for His return.

Remember, we also are not our own.

> "Or do you not know that your body is the temple of the Holy Spirit *who is* in you, whom you have from God, and <u>you are not your own?</u>
>
> For you were bought at a [blood] price; therefore, glorify God in your body and your spirit, which are God's."
> -1 Corinthians 6:19,20

This kind of life can only be achieved by making day-to-day decisions on how we should conduct ourselves in a manner worthy of His absence.

> "Therefore, as *the* <u>elect</u> (*chosen*) of God, holy and beloved, put on tender mercies, kindness, humility, meekness, longsuffering;
>
> bearing with one another, and forgiving one another, if anyone has a complaint against another; even as Christ forgave you, so you also *must* do.
>
> But above all these things put on love, which is the <u>bond of perfection</u> (*state of completion*)."
> -Colossians 3:12-14

When Jesus was with His disciples in the upper room, with the absence of Judas, He had much to say and so little time to say it. What He shared with them and what He shares with us now can only be in the hearing of someone who truly desires to imitate their Bridegroom as a faithful Kallah should, according to Jewish tradition and custom.

> "A <u>new</u> [a different way of life] commandment I give to you, that you love one another; [meaning] **AS I have loved you**, that you also love one another.
>
> By this all will know that you are My disciples, **IF** you have love for one another.
> -John 13:34,35

Here's a question that I bet you never considered-: what if Jesus loved us, just AS we have loved and have shown love towards others?

It should NEVER matter how we are treated, only that we stay the same in how we treat others, this is the way of our Bridegroom.

Why should I treat someone as they have treated me? Would I then not become the very person they are? I am not saying that I have mastered this way of life, for no one can fully emulate love as perfectly as Jesus did.

However, our Ketubah (_____) encourages us-

> "And let us not grow weary while doing good, for in due season we <u>shall reap</u> [the good that we have sown] **IF** we do not lose heart.
>
> Therefore, as we have opportunity, let us do good to all, especially to those <u>who are of the household</u> of faith (*the children of His household*)."
> -Galatians 6:9,10

I believe Paul captures the heart of our Bridegroom when He says-

> "For to me, to live is Christ, and to die is gain."
> -Philippians 1:21

Back to John 13:35, Jesus wasn't saying we would not be His disciples if we didn't show love. But rather, how would anyone know we were His disciples, or brides for that matter, if we imitated the world instead of trying to emulate Him.

> "....as He who called you *is* holy, you also be holy in all your conduct,
>
> because it is written, *"Be holy, for I am holy."*
> -1 Peter 1:15,16 (*ref*: Lev. 11:44, 45; 19:2; 20:7)

If you truly desire to fully live the life that your

Bridegroom desires for you, you must take the time to read your Ketubah, commit it to memory, and trust His sayings.

📖 As a betrothed bride, her first priority would be to find a **Mikvah** (*a large gathering of water*) where she would immerse herself. The source of this water had to be living water, either from a natural stream or from fresh rainwater.

This immersion is done to symbolize her new state of being sanctified, holy, and set apart for her bridegroom, as he would have made it a precedence to do the same. In today's modern culture, we call it being baptized. 📖

As Believers, I believe the very moment that we accept Jesus into our hearts, we instantaneously go through a spiritual baptism.

> "Or do you not know that as many of us as were baptized (*fully immersed*) in Christ Jesus were baptized (*fully immersed*) in his death?
>
> Therefore, we were buried with Him through baptism [being fully immersed] in death, that just as Christ was raised from the dead by the glory of the Father, even so we also should walk in newness of life.
> -Romans 6:3,4

Also, Paul writes-

> "For you are all sons (*a place of position not gender*) of God through faith in Christ Jesus.
>
> For as many of you as were baptized into Christ

have put on Christ.

> There is neither Jews nor Greek (*Gentile*), there is neither slave nor free, there is neither male nor female; for you are all one in Christ Jesus.
> -Galatians 3:26-28

Though we have indeed gone through a spiritual baptism, our Bridegroom, Jesus, still requires us to seek out a pool of water and be baptized in the name of God the Father, God the Son, and God the Holy Spirit (Matthew 28:19).

And if He required His bride to do so, then it would stand to reason that He also would have had to get baptized as well. John the Baptist had the honor of doing this.

> "It came to pass in those days that Jesus came from Nazareth of Galilee and was baptized by John in the Jordan (*a Mikvah*).
>
> And immediately, coming up from the water, He saw the heavens parting and the Spirit descending upon Him like a dove.
>
> Then a voice came from heaven, "You are my beloved Son, in whom I am well pleased."
> -Mark 1:9-11

Are you beginning to see how every step of the way Jesus has followed this ancient tradition to the letter? And we, as His bride, get to experience this same amazing journey!

📖 Continuing with her small to-do list-

- She would make her own wedding gown of fine linen, adorned with shells, pomegranates, jewelry, and whatever else she might have on hand. If need be, she would use the **Mattanah** (_____) given to her by her bridegroom or if her father was a generous man, he would share with her the **mohar** (_____) he received for her payment.

- She would make sure she had plenty of oil for her lamp and that her wicks were trimmed and ready for the journey.

- She would choose her bridesmaids and oversee their progress in preparing for the event; each one had to be committed and ready at a moment's notice for the journey ahead.

From reading Psalms 45 it is believed that these bridesmaids were virgins and not betrothed or married women.

> "The royal daughter is all glorious within the palace; Her clothing is woven with gold.
>
> She shall be brought to the King in robes of many colors; the virgins, her companions who follow her, shall be brought to You.
>
> With gladness and rejoicing they shall be brought; they shall enter the King's palace."
>
> -Psalm 45:13-15

Considering of course, that a young woman who was betrothed would be too busy preparing herself for her bridegroom, and a married woman would simply be too occupied with her own responsibilities of managing her own children and household.

Though it was the responsibility of the bride to choose her bridesmaids carefully, it was ultimately their own responsibility to be prepared at a moment's notice: their lamp ready, wicks trimmed, plenty of oil, and dresses decorated for the wedding procession.

The bridegrooms most often came at night and the only illumination that was offered was from the small handheld lamp that gave off just enough light for the young girls to be able to see what was directly in front of them.

The streets around that time were narrow with twists and turns. If you ran out of oil and had to stop along the way, you could miss the procession and be left behind (See- Matt. 25:1-13). This too sounds a bit familiar, doesn't it? 📖

We as brothers and sisters in Christ are more closely related by His blood that flows through our veins, than we are to our own flesh and blood. However, who you choose to surround yourself with, and who you choose to listen to, will most certainly help in shaping your life, whether good or bad. You will either influence others or they will influence you.

You have heard it said, "you are who you hang around with."

> "He who walks with [the] wise <u>men</u> (*mankind*), will be wise, but the companion of fools will be destroyed."
>
> -Proverbs 13:20

In other words, choose your bridesmaids (friends) carefully

> "I have been crucified with Christ; it is no longer I who live, but Christ lives in me; and the life which I now [choose] to live in the flesh I live by faith in the Son of God, who loved me and gave Himself for me.
> -Galatians 2:20

Therefore-

> "... put off, concerning your former conduct, the old man which grows corrupt, according to the deceitful lusts (*strong desires*),
>
> and be renewed in the spirit of your mind
>
> and that you put on the new man which was created according to God, in true righteousness and holiness."
> -Ephesians 4:22-24

📖 Whenever she went out in the community, she was expected to wear a **Tza'iph** (*veil*). Her face would be hidden, except for her eyes, showing that she was no longer available to receive offers of marriage. (This makes me wonder if veils might have been handed down from generation to generation as some precious items still are today from mother to daughter.)

The veil indicated that she was promised to someone in betrothment. And she would wear this veil whenever she was out in public, until the night he uncovers her in the Bridal Chamber.

Back then, you could tell a lot about a Jewish woman by the way they were dressed, or the way they wore their hair out in public.

- If a young girl's head was uncovered, you can safely assume that she was available for marriage.

- If you saw a young girl with a head covering and a veil, she was legally betrothed and no longer available to receive any other offers.

- If you saw a woman with her hair up and covered, you could be certain that she was a married woman and to approach her would be a huge mistake.

Interestingly enough, in the Talmudic period, circa 70CE, a husband could legally divorce his wife if she was caught without wearing a head covering. (*ref:* jewishvirtuallibrary.org/covering-of-the-head)

The veil represented a woman's marital status very much like rings are today. An engagement ring on a modern woman's finger would mean that she is engaged to another and is unavailable, a wedding band would signify that she is married and should be respected as such, and no ring would simply mean she is available- at least that is how it is supposed to be.

With her veil in place, she is ready to go out and share her good news. However, she wouldn't need to say anything, the veil would speak for itself.

Now let us check in on the bridegroom. I promise you will be so happy that you are the girl in this story.

"In My Father's house are many [exquisite] rooms, if it were not so, I would have told you. And if I go to prepare a place for you, I will come again and receive you to Myself; that where I am, you may be also."

-John 14:2,3

The Chupah

The Bridal Chamber

In today's western culture, it is the bride who runs around like a chicken with its head cut off trying to get everything done before the day of the wedding. The bridegroom, well he only needs to have his suit ready, secure the rings, and choose his best man. But trust me when I tell you that our bridegroom in this love story will not just be sitting around twirling his thumbs, waiting for the days, weeks, and months to pass by.

📖 Every detail leading up to the day of his return rests ceremonially on his shoulders. The **chatan** (*bridegroom*) alone held the burden of making sure everything was in place before he was permitted to retrieve his bride. Primarily this would include building a solid structure from the ground up that would connect to his father's house for them to dwell in and raise a family.

Under the auspices and strict eyes of his father, it would be the sole responsibility of the son to build this room and, may I add, with no help from anyone else.

Because I absolutely love biblical history, this got me thinking about what a typical Jewish home would look like. In the time of Jesus, it was very common for entire families to live together under one household: father, mother, unmarried daughters, sons with their wives and children. Even possibly aunts and uncles would all live together under one roof.

A wealthy Jewish family would usually have a two-story home. There would be an open courtyard in the central part of the residence that was used as a multipurpose area. Families would frequently gather there for meals cooked over an open fire, a time of prayer and worship, and the occasional entertainment of music and storytelling. Connected to the Courtyard would be several rooms off to the side for storage, supplies, and a kitchen of sorts.

Most homes would also have a room strictly for the livestock to settle in for the night, so that they may be protected from predators and harsh weather elements. The upper room would be used as their sleeping quarters.

On the roof was usually where much of the household chores were done; spinning wool or cotton to make clothes, grinding grain such as barley and wheat, washing clothes and then hanging them out to dry over the railing, and sometimes they would even sleep on the rooftop if it was just too unbearable to sleep indoors due to the summer weather.

The average Jewish family would most likely have a one-story home with a much smaller courtyard and rooms built off the side for various purposes as explained above. Only the poorest of families would have just one, possibly two rooms to live in with a slightly upper level. This raised floor was used for meal preparation and performing everyday activities. If the weather did not permit them to sleep on the roof, they would use this upper level as their sleeping quarters. At night, if they had small livestock, they would bring them inside to which they would stay on the lower level of the home.

Now let's assume that our chatan (_____) is from a middle-class family. An area off the courtyard would be chosen, measured off and a trench would be dug before construction could even begin. He would place four foundational cornerstones that had to be the same size and dimension for stability and be able to anchor the supporting walls. The walls had to be thick enough to have small alcoves carved out to store sleeping mats, clothes, and supplies.

The type of stone that he would use for the walls would depend largely on where he lived. In the central area of Israel, white limestone was used to build homes (this type of stone was used to build Herod's Temple). He also might have made available to him sedimentary stones, or rough stones that were pieced together like a puzzle, mortared with mud and straw.

If he lived in an area that did not have these types of stones, he could use mud bricks made from dirt, water and straw then dried in the sun. Another type of brick and mortar could be clay mixed with broken shells and potsherds. All these choices just depended on what he had accessible to him and what he could afford.

After he finished the walls, the roof was added on. It needed to be heavily supported by strong timber that stretched across each side in order to provide the needed support; it had to hold the weight of everyday activities that went on. The ceiling floor was made with straw mats and overlaid with clay. Unlike our homes today, the roofs had to be repaired yearly due to harsh weather conditions that Israel was known for.

There even was a law put in place to encompass the roof's edge with a railing for the safety of the people.

> "When you build a new house, then you shall make a parapet for your roof, so that you may not bring guilt of bloodshed on your household if anyone falls from it."
>
> -Deuteronomy 22:8

Every day his father would come and inspect his work and if any of the work was done improperly or put together haphazardly, his father would have him tear it down and start over. After all, this new edition would be connected to his fathers' house and could affect the soundness of the whole building.

It was important that he took his time and did it perfectly the first go around. Otherwise, time and materials would be wasted.

Because the bridegroom also had family duties that he was responsible for, he could only work on the room during his free time. This would explain why it would have taken him so long before he could retrieve his bride.

When he finished the roof, he then worked on the floor, leveling it out and pounding it down flat. Wealthy homeowners would lay down pebbled floors or clay tiles, and the very wealthy were able to install wood flooring.

By this time, close to a year has gone by now and he must be feeling the anticipation of returning for his bride. However, only the father knows the day and hour to which he will release him, and I think it is safe to say that he will not let his son go until the smallest detail has been completed. He will accept nothing less than perfection. Once the father approves of the construction of the room, phase one is complete and phase two is then set in motion: the furnishings.

For decorations, he would probably hang dried flowers, palm leaves, and dried herbs from the ceiling for a sweet fragrance. He would make the bed and pillows out of straw, cotton, or wool and have plenty of fresh linens; after all, that would be the most important area in the whole room.

He would have several lamps for lighting with extra vessels of oil, and scented candles, if he could afford them.

For provisions, he would bring in large water containers for hygiene uses, vessel jars of wine, and enough food to last the seven days that they would be spending alone such as: loaves of wheat and barley, olives, fresh figs, various kinds of vegetables, fruits and nuts, and whatever else he can think of to make their experience memorable.

Finally, it is finished! The son watches his father closely as he gives a final inspection of the room. With an eagle's eye he looks over the completed construction of the entire room, inside and out: the strength of the walls, the levelness of the floor, and the stability of the roof.

He then inspects the décor of the room, making sure it is as charming as possible. Finally, he slowly scans the room, looking over all the provisions needed for their seven-day stay. He might even make some suggestions of items his son has forgotten to bring in if needed. (I always imagine the father taking just a few extra moments before giving his blessing just to make his son squirm a bit).

And then turning towards him, he offers a proud nod of approval and in the blink of an eye, the bridegroom is off and running!

Putting on his wedding attire, he grabs his **Shofar** (*rams' horn*), and runs out to gather his friends together; making sure that everyone has their lamps and plenty of oil for the journey there and back.

With his friends and best man by his side, they would begin the procession towards her father's house. More times than not, it would be the dead of night and she would have no idea he was coming for her! 📖

Imagine if you will........

A Tale of Unimaginable Love

It is the dead of night. She is awakened by the sharp blast of a Shofar and loud shouts from just a short distance away, he has come!

Wiping the sleep from her eyes, she lights a small lamp by her bed and quickly hurries to get dressed. She is so nervous; she can barely tie the linen cord of her wedding gown around the back of her neck. Next, she reaches for her lace head covering and tucks in any loose hair she might have, then sits on her bed to put on her newly made sandals; she must hurry, she knows she doesn't have much time!

Except for the silk veil that had been passed down from mother to daughter for generations, everything she is wearing was made with her own hands. Lastly, she shoves a small lamp and extra vessels of oil into a small leather pouch and places it across her shoulder.

Standing in her modest two room home, she takes a moment to do a mental check from head to toe: head covering is in place, sandals are tied, and the pouch with her lamp and oil, she is ready. Smoothing down her gown she takes a deep breath, forcing herself to let it out slowly. "Oh! My veil!" She reaches for her veil that had been delicately folded by her bed, taking great care to put it on, now she is ready!

Rushing to ready themselves, some of her bridesmaids were not prepared and began voicing their concerns for not having enough oil in their vessels when suddenly the door bursts open, and several young men come rushing in unapologetically, waking her whole family with resounding shouts of joy!

In their recklessness, they don't even notice that they had just knocked over a table with a full pitcher of water that now lay spilled on the floor.

Her father jolts up in bed at the abrupt intrusion going on in his home. Trying to focus in on the commotion that is taking place, he throws the covers off determined to defend his family when he feels his wife's soft but firm hand on his back. He turns to look at her as she smiles and beckons him to lie back down next to her.

Looking back at the chaos and again at his wife, he realizes that the bridegroom has come for his daughter. Bittersweet emotions of joy mixed with the sadness of losing her begin to fill his heart all at once. Now he knows how his father-in-law must have felt when he took his betrothed bride from his home.

Reaching for his wife's hand, he lays back down and stares at the ceiling; he couldn't watch his precious daughter leave his home for the last time.

In the commotion, she presses herself up against a corner of the room watching as the young men find her bridesmaids huddling together, screaming out with joy as the men come in like thieves in the night catching them away. But not one of them will lay a hand on her, for she is his alone!

In what seemed like a blink of an eye, they are all gone, and the room becomes very quiet. Overwhelming anticipation began to course through her body. She has been a bridesmaid a few times but never a bride; this time he is coming for her!

He enters the room hesitating for just a few moments to adjust his eyes to the low-lit room. Searching, he sees her in the far corner; she is absolutely breathtaking! He had been waiting for this day for what seemed like an eternity and finally that day had arrived! He had been in such a hurry to get here that he must resist the urge to seize her right then and there. Taking a deep breath, he makes slow deliberate steps towards her until he is standing within reach.

He is so close, she can feel his breath cool upon her skin, his clothes lightly smelling of frankincense and myrrh. She didn't realize how tall he was until he stood towering over her small frame.

When he came to her father's house a little over a year ago, she would barely look at him as her father read her Ketubah before the whole family. Only when he handed her the cup, they would share together did she glance up to see his face. She remembered feeling unworthy to receive such an offer and that there were so many other girls who were prettier and far better than herself, and yet, he chose her.

Looking at him now, she notices that his dark brown hair has a slight wave to it as it lay just past his shoulders, and his well-trimmed beard seemed so soft, she is tempted to reach up and run her fingers through it but dares not! He had a smile that was warm and inviting but it was the smile in his eyes that now seemed to capture her attention.

He reaches for her, tucking a wisp of hair back inside her laced head covering, purposely taking his time as he caresses her cheek.

All that he gave to obtain this beautiful young woman who stood before him now was worth the extravagant price that he so willingly paid.

"I told you that I would come for you", he said, smiling down on her. She couldn't think, she couldn't breathe; her heart was beating so fast in her chest. She could only stare silently, mesmerized by those fiery eyes of golden brown that held her gaze with such intensity. He doesn't wait for her response as he firmly picks her up in his arms and carries her to the door.

He has no intention of waiting for her father's permission, nor does he look his way; he has paid a great price for his beloved and he shall have what is his.

Setting her back on her feet just outside the door, he reaches for her hand and begins to lead her in the direction of her new home. She tries to look back, hoping to get a glimpse of her parents one more time but feels his hand lightly squeezing hers; reminding her that her life is ahead now and not behind her.

Though the journey was long, time seemed to disappear as they approached his father's kingdom. Sounds of merriment began to fill the air as they entered through the massive gates that protected the entrance. Everywhere she looked, the streets were filled with people of various cultures, races, and ethnicities. "The king's son has arrived," they shouted, and he has his bride!" They begin to gather around her, welcoming her with hugs and kisses on her cheeks.

She was so elated by their welcome that she wanted to stay a little while, wanting to know who they were. But when she began to resist his leading, only then did he stop and turns towards her.

"There will be plenty of time for you to spend with your new friends and family," he said hurriedly, "but we must continue." And with another slight squeeze of her hand that gave no room to protest, they continued towards the massive house located in the center of the kingdom.

As they entered his father's house, she is overwhelmed at the celebration of their arrival, captivated by the breathtaking view that lay before her. There were so many people in the outer courtyard that it was impossible to count them. She sees her bride-maids in the distance, but she only counted five. "Where are the others, did they lose their way?"

Her thoughts are interrupted as her bridegroom introduces her to his father. "Welcome my daughter, welcome to your new home, all that I have is yours," he proclaims as he takes her in his arms and kisses her forehead. "Everything you see has been prepared for you alone!"

Friends of his father are not waiting to be introduced, they too are excited to meet the daughter-in-law he had been talking about since the day his son was betrothed. They all greet her with open arms, welcoming her with great joy.

There is so much to see! In the center of the courtyard where she entered, was a huge banquet table that stood from one end of the courtyard clear across to the other side with every kind of food imaginable. In all the wedding ceremonies she has attended, she has not seen such provision made for a wedding feast and all of this was in her honor!

There is music playing and people everywhere are dancing, laughing, and trying to talk above the music to be heard. She has barely enough time to take it all in before he puts his hand on the small of her back leading her towards the Bridal Chamber. He will not wait any longer.

As they enter in, he firmly closes the door behind them, shutting out the loud sounds of music and laughter; it's just the two of them now. He takes a few steps back, attentively watching as she experiences her new surroundings.

The entire place is lit with sweet-scented candles. As she stands in the middle of the room, she is amazed that it was almost as big as her father's house! Moving consciously about the room, she takes in the fragrant aroma of fresh cut flowers, oils of frankincense and myrrh, and even hints of fresh baked bread sitting on a table against the wall along with baskets of assorted fruits and vegetables. Standing beside the table sits several large vats of wine.

She looks up to find hanging shells of various shapes and sizes, palm branches and dried herbs. Tears begin to well up in her eyes, she can't help but feel overjoyed that he would so carefully take the time to make sure the room, their room, would be so perfect.

Tucked aptly away in another corner are several large containers of water for washing with fresh linens nearby. As she continues to study her surroundings, she notices two small open windows up near the ceiling to let just enough light and fresh air in. She notices that the walls have several niches, and she smiles to herself as she begins to imagine what she would store in each one. Though she knows she will have plenty of time to acclimatize herself to her new surroundings, still, she wanted to take in every detail. This is her new home, and she couldn't be more pleased.

Turning, she is suddenly aware of the bedding covered with fine linens and several pillows resting against the wall.

Her heart begins to race and suddenly she is aware that he is standing just a few feet away. She doesn't realize that he has been steadily watching her, patiently waiting for her to take it all in.

Their eyes finally meet, "it is the most beautiful room I have ever seen; I can't believe you did all this for me," she says nervously, afraid to say anything else. He, however, doesn't say a word but makes His way towards her. Nothing matters to Him now except this time, here, with her.

A gentle breeze is felt in the room from the windows above and unexpectantly he catches the scent of her sweet fragrant perfume. Closing his eyes, he pauses as he slowly takes a deep breath in, lingering there as long as possible before slowly exhaling.

"Do not be in a hurry", he reminds himself again, "take your time, she is yours now". Opening his eyes, he continues to move towards her, until he is standing so close, it forces her to look up at him.

Brushing her cheeks with his hands as he slides her head covering off revealing long jet-black hair that cascaded to the middle of her back. Not being able to help himself, he reaches for thick strands of hair and takes in mixed fragrances of Galbanum and Rose of Sharon, his favorite scent.

He then reaches for her veil, revealing soft lips that he has been so longingly wanting to touch with his own. He moves his hand through her hair, just under the base of her neck and softly pulls her to him, touching her lips with his own.

He has desired this young woman ever since he met her family while traveling to Jerusalem to celebrate the annual Passover. He remembered the day as if it was yesterday when he approached his father and asked him to approve the betrothment between him and this beautiful woman standing before him. He was willing to give all that to obtain her as his own.

Keeping her in his close embrace, he reaches for the bow at the base of her neck and deliberately pulls until it loosens, causing her gown to fall to the floor unhindered.

Suddenly she realizes that she is naked, and her eyes fall to the floor. Her body tenses up, afraid he might not be pleased. "What if he is unhappy with her, what if he changes his mind, I couldn't bear it if" .... her thoughts are interrupted.

"Look at me," he says lifting her chin up, forcing her to look into eyes that were gentle but demanded attention. "I have been waiting for this night with great anticipation, you must know that you are beautiful in my sight. Do not hide your eyes from me, my love, for I have loved you with an everlasting love that will not be quenched, nor will it ever fade away. You will always be mine as I am forever yours."

And as he pulls her closer still, all the fears of rejection, apprehension, and doubt begin to fade away as she is embraced in his perfect love that knows no boundaries. Waves of unimaginable emotions begin to wash over her;

feeling his love surrounding her, she relaxes in his embrace.

Not being able to wait any longer, he picks her up and carries her to their bed. As he lays her down, he slowly reaches for ...

"He who has the bride is the bridegroom; but the friend of the bridegroom, who stands and hears him, rejoices greatly because of the bridegroom's voice."

-John 3:29

The Chatan

The Bridegroom

📖 There are some who believe that the **Betrothal Ceremony** (presenting the Ketubah, paying the mohar, and sharing the sefel) was a festive time and done in public. However, nowhere in scripture does it mention or describe a public marriage ceremony like we have today.

I believe that the proceedings were very discreet and done in the privacy of the potential bride's home, as was the betrothment done between Isaac and Rebekah; Jacob and Leah; and again, with Rachel.

As we continue to follow this ancient tradition, the bridegroom would come at a time that was unexpected, and almost always at night. He, with his full entourage, would ascend upon her home just moments after the blast of the shofar and loud shouts of their arrival. 📖

One day soon, our Lord will also come for His bride when it is least expected-

> "For you yourselves know perfectly that the day of the Lord so come as a thief in the night."
> -1 Thessalonians 5:2

Paul also tells us-

> "For this we say to you by the word of the Lord, that we who are alive and remain [here on earth] until the coming of the Lord, will by no means precede those who are asleep [and have gone home before us].
>
> For the Lord Himself will descend from heaven with a shout, with the voice of an archangel, and with the trumpet of God, and the dead in Christ will rise first.
>
> Then we who are <u>alive</u> (*living now*) and remain [here on earth] **shall be caught up** together with them in the clouds to meet the Lord [our Bridegroom] in the air. And thus, we shall always be with the Lord."
> -1 Thessalonians 4:15-17

Do you remember this scripture from a previous chapter? It is definitely worth repeating. These four words, "shall be caught up" is the Greek word, "*harpazo*" (726 Strongs Concordance) and it can mean- "*to catch away, to be plucked, or to take by force.*" It can also mean to snatch or take away from one place to another.

This same word "*harpazo*" is also used to describe Phillips experience in Acts 8:39, and the Apostle Paul's experience in 2 Corinthians 12:2-4.

And unlike our bride in this story, who would have had only a few moments to ready herself and prepare for his arrival, we will not have that luxury.

Our preparation period is in the here and now, for our Bridegroom will come in a blink of an eye (1/100 of a second), and there will be no time to prepare.

> "Behold, I tell you a mystery (*a revealed secret*): We shall not all sleep (*die*), but we shall be changed-
>
> in a moment, in the twinkling of an eye, at the last trumpet. For the trumpet will sound, and the dead (*those who have gone before us*) will be raised incorruptible and we [who are living on the earth] shall be [forever] changed."
>
> -1 Corinthians 15:51,52

With no warning, our Bridegroom will also one day soon come for His bride.

She and her bridesmaids will most likely be traveling in the dead of night and all they will have for a light is a small lamp that will guide their way.

At last, they will arrive at his father's house where his guests will be waiting to receive them in a congratulatory manner. However, she will have very little time to meet everyone for she will be ushered into the Bridal Chamber where she will stay for 7 days. There they will consummate their marriage.

After **nissuin** (*consummation*) is complete, the bridegroom will go to the door where the best man is waiting and announce that they have completed nissuin. It might seem odd, but it was traditional for the bride to keep the linen that showed the evidence of her losing her virginity in case her husband decides to reject her and say she was not a virgin when he received her. I'm assuming that God had foreseen this happening and had decreed a law to protect the young girl from shame (*Deut. 22:13-21*).

Getting back to the party, the best man will have announced the good news to the guests and the wedding festivities would then begin in quite a celebratory fashion with loud music, dancing, and lots of eating and drinking. It was the responsibility of the bridegroom to have an ample supply of wine for their wedding guests. And so, it was absolutely unheard of to run out of food and especially wine as was the case with Jesus in Cana.

His mother, Mary, was trying to save the bridegroom from a pending disaster by approaching her Son when the Master of the Feast ran out of wine. Though it was not Jesus' time, I believe the love of His mother is what compelled Him to intercede and by doing so, saved the family from shame and embarrassment (John 2:1-10).

What is so interesting about this, is that by Jesus being the one who supplied the wine, puts Him in the position of the bridegroom. I truly believe the wine He supplied that day came directly from the vineyards in Heaven. And one day soon, we will know what that wine tasted like as it too will be served to us in the Great Hall of our Father's kingdom when we will all sit at our Bridegroom's table.

The celebration can last for days on end, right up to the receiving of the bride and bridegroom coming out of the Bridal Chamber on the seventh day.

Though the celebration was going on outside, both bride and bridegroom were expected to stay in their Bridal Chamber for the duration of the 7 days; this would give them time to get more acquainted with one another.

At the end of their 7 days, they would emerge out of the Bridal Chamber and be greeted by all the guests who have been anxiously waiting to receive them and a great feast would be prepared in their honor. 📖

In my research, I have read several commentaries and blogs that gave different perspectives on whether the bridegroom stays with her in the room or, do they both come in and out throughout the seven days of being in the Bridal Chamber. But I have found from experience that when in doubt, go to the Author where the truth lies, waiting to be found.

The answer is found in Genesis 29. We see it played out between Jacob, Leah, and Rachel. Here's the long and short of it.

> Jacob was living with his uncle, Laban, and fell in love with his youngest daughter Rachel. He approached Laban with a Ketubah and an agreed price of seven

years of labor. Laban agreed and they were legally betrothed. When Jacob finished out the seven years, he expected to complete the **nissuin** (*consummated*) with Rachel. However, Laban brought Leah to him and because she was veiled which was the custom, Jacob took her into the Bridal Chamber and consummated with her.

In v.25-28 we read that Jacob got a huge surprise when he woke up the next morning and it was Leah beside him and not his love, Rachel. I think it is safe to say he had a conniption fit and left the Bridal Chamber to confront his uncle.

Laban told Jacob that it was not their custom to allow the younger sister to marry before the older one (which would have been nice if he was told that little bit of detail), and so encouraged him to complete Leah's week in the Bridal Chamber. Afterwards, he would then give Rachel to him for the agreed service of another seven years. To which reluctantly, he did.

Most of us have heard the story taught in such a way that would give the impression that Jacob had to work for another seven years *before* receiving Rachel as his wife. If we read the scriptures closely, Jacob took Rachel into the Bridal Chamber as soon as he fulfilled the required seven days with his first wife, Leah. Laban then gave his daughter, Rachel to him.

Remember, Jacob's first seven years of service was a legal payment for Rachel, not Leah; but because He completed **nissuin** with Leah, he was legally bound to her.

Jacob could have legally divorced Leah because of Laban's deceit but if he did so, he would have caused great shame to her. As we can see, Jacob was a man of honor.

I once watched a Jewish wedding on YouTube. A bride, with her face veiled, was walking down the aisle with her father in hand. Just short of the altar, they stopped to wait on the bridegroom, who then walked up to her and lifted her veil. I couldn't help but chuckle when I realized that he was making sure that she was the one to whom he was to be betrothed to before he escorted her underneath the Chupah. I can only imagine Jacob doing the same; you know the saying, "fool me once shame on you, fool me twice..."

There you have it! An ancient traditional Jewish marriage ceremony from beginning to end, was placed solely on the bridegrooms' shoulders: writing out the Katubah, the price he paid, the gifts he gave, the home he built, and the preparations he made for their life together. And yet, for him, it was all about the girl.

The more you read your own Ketubah, the more you will begin to see what a romantic our Bridegroom really is and how He longs to come for His bride. Which begs the question, "what is God waiting for?" This is not a mystery; Peter reveals God's heart in his second letter.

> "The Lord is not <u>slack</u> (*delay, tarry*) concerning His promise [of return], as some count slackness, but is <u>longsuffering</u> (*patient*) toward us, not willing that any <u>should perish</u> (*be destroyed*) but that all should come to <u>repentance</u> (*a change of mind*)."

-2 Peter 3:9

He loves you and that neighbor of yours that gets on your nerves. He loves your friends that you are trying to minister to and that co-worker that talks behind your back. He loves your family members that you're praying for and that family member that you wouldn't care if you ever saw them again. He is patient towards them all.

> "But the day of the Lord will come as a thief in the night, in which the heavens will pass away with a great noise, and the elements will melt (*disintegrate*) with fervent heat; both the earth and the works that are in it will be burned up (*laid bare*)."
>
> -2 Peter 3:10

He is coming, will you be found ready?

> "Therefore, beloved, look forward (*anticipate*) to these things, be diligent (*labor, make effort*) to be found by Him in peace, without spot and blameless;
>
> and consider that the longsuffering (*patience*) of our Lord is salvation [to those who do not yet know Him]- ..."
>
> -2 Peter 3:14,15a

A Personal Letter From Your Bridegroom

My Beloved Bride,

You have read the parable about the kingdom of heaven is like a merchant seeking beautiful pearls, that when he found one of great price, went and sold all that he had and bought it. You, My love, are that pearl of great price!

When I breathe you in, I am brought in remembrance of the sweet-smelling fragrance that exudes from the life you have lived since the day you accepted Me as your Bridegroom. I witnessed all of heaven rejoicing the day you took from the cup of salvation.

Though you may not think that you have anything to offer, I assure you that the life you have given Me is priceless. You have been My choice bride from the beginning of time, and I have NEVER been disappointed in you, nor have I EVER regretted joining My life with yours.

My Father is overseeing all of heaven-preparations are being made ready for your arrival, the Bridal Chamber is almost complete, and the Wedding Feast is being prepared. There is a stirring of excitement beginning to take place in My Father's house, and you have friends and family here waiting for you.

Though there are many in My Fathers kingdom, I want you to know that I see you! You are not lost in the assembly of brides that He has chosen for Me, I know who you are! You are loved individually and independently from all others and even though you stand in the company of them, I see you!

In your worship, you will find Me listening to the sweet sound of your voice; in your praise, you will hear Me speak words of love and affirmation to you; and in your prayers, you will see Me continually moving in your midst, working all things out for your good.

Therefore, make a daily decision to set your mind on things that are above and not on the things of the earth, for I am your life now and you are hidden in Me.

Do not allow yourself to be stuck in the muck and mire of this life and its worldly desires. Rather be the light in the darkness; be the city that is set on a high hill for all to see; be the salt of the earth, so that in the midst of your trouble the world will see your steadfast love and faithfulness towards Me and rejoice with you when you are delivered out.

Remember always, My love, that You are My most holy possession and are loved beyond measure. Soon I will come to claim you as My own. But until then, know that you are ever before Me and I am in constant anticipation for the day that I can hold you in My arms, see you face to face and say, 'Well done My beloved, well done.'

Until that day is realized, wait patiently for Me, for I am coming soon, and on that Day, you will appear with Me in My Father's kingdom. You are the praise of My glory.

*Your Beloved Bridegroom,
Jesus*

Love Notes

From You

Love Notes

Love Notes

Appendix

A Nation is Born
— Israel

A Marriage Covenant of Laws Broken
— Israel's Katubah

More About Our Shadchan

More About The Cup

More About The Mikvah

The Veil

The Shofar

> Note: To keep the main story concise and engaging, I chose to include an appendix for some of the earlier chapters. This way, I can provide additional information without overwhelming the narrative.
>
> As you read these chapters, you may encounter some repetition, such as the reuse of scriptures or the retelling of specific parts of the story.

"Now the Lord said to Abram: 'Get out of your country, from your family and from your father's house to a land that I will show you. And I will make you a great nation.'"

-Genesis 12:1,2

A Nation is Born - Israel

The Story of Abram and Sarai

Abram was seventy-five years old when God called him out of the land of Haran. This amazing adventure that Abram was about to embark on, was led solely by his faith in God's word. Regardless of whether Abram felt joy, apprehension, fear, excitement, or trepidation, he still packed up all that was his and began the journey to a place God told him to go.

We know that Abram, at the time, had no heirs. It is probable that the promise of an heir was strong enough to push through any apprehension he might have had to leave his country, his family, and his father's house (Gen. 12:1).

This leap of faith in God's word, would lead him into unfamiliar territory he had never been, encountering inhabitants of various cultures he knew nothing about, and facing confrontations he had never experienced before; all because God said, "*get out*."

Oh, to have the simple faith of Abram! To go when God says, "*go*" and to stay when God says, "*stay*," without a detailed explanation, four prophetic words and five confirmations.

Studying the first few verses of Genesis 12 made me realize that I can sometimes be the child that God would have to tell *way* in advance to move in any one direction. And though I might tend to move slower than others, the point is, I'm still moving.

> "He who calls you is faithful, who also will do it."
> -1 Thessalonians 5:24

It used to bother me when I would hear about someone who had moved on a word from God without thought or strategy, because they trusted God to do the rest. And I, on the other side of the pendulum, would seem to move at a snail's pace because I needed details and a strategy.

A few years ago, I was talking with a friend of mine and she was sharing with me about her plans to move to another state in the next month and start a ministry, I asked her when He told her this and she said, "just last week."

I remember feeling disheartened that she would be so brave to just get up and go when I too believed that God spoke to me about a ministry, however, I was moving at a much slower pace. I hardly paid attention to what she said afterwards as I was beginning to feel defeated, and that God would probably pass me by because I was moving too slow.

When I got into my car, God immediately spoke to me-

> Caren- if I had a project that needed to be done at a specific time, I would tell Angela days before, because I know she would not hesitate to move forward when I need her to.
>
> If I needed you to move on the same day, I would tell you months in advance, because I also know you, in how you think, and process things. And I know you will do it when I need it done. Caren, you're not missing Me, you're right on time.

These words bring me in remembrance once again of all that He has done and all the promises He has made and kept through my faithfulness to follow His lead.

God doesn't care about the pace you're setting; He already knows how long it will take for you to achieve the work and has planned accordingly, you just keep moving forward. This year, 2024, is our seventh year in ministry -Bride of Christ Encounter- and we are continuing to impact the lives of so many women.

Abram's journey should be an encouragement to us all as we continue our faith walk and trust God in the direction He is leading. And should we need affirmations along the way, I promise, He will always be there to reassure us through His word.

> "God is not a man, that He would lie, nor a son of man, that He would change His mind; Has he

> said, and will He not do it? Or has He spoken, and will He not make it good?"
>
> -Numbers. 23:19

Now Abram might not have known all the intricacies of God's plan, but <u>he believed</u> that God spoke to him, <u>he trusted</u> His promises (Gen.12:1-3), and by faith <u>he moved</u>. And when he passed through the land of Canaan to the place of Shechem, the Lord appeared to him and said, "to your descendants I will give this land" (*v.*12:6,7).

And when Lot and Abram parted company (*v.*13:11), God spoke to Abram a second time regarding the land of Canaan that his descendants would inherit.

> "and the Lord said to Abram, after Lot had separated from him: 'Lift your eyes now and look from the place where you are- northward, southward, eastward, and westward; for all the land which you see <u>I give to you</u> and your descendants forever.'"
>
> -Genesis 13:14,15

God did not say, "I <u>will</u> give to you" as if Abram had to wait for it, He was telling Abram, "I have already given it to you." This time, God was speaking directly to Abram, calling those things which do not exist as though they did and expected Abram to see the land as if it already belonged to him, filled with descendants he did not have.

> "Arise, walk in the land through its length and its width, for <u>I give it to you</u>."
>
> -Genesis 13:17

Abram did what the Lord said (*v.*13:18). And through his obedience, not only did he become the father of a great nation, but he also became a father to all nations who would call on the name of the Lord!

Can you imagine standing in one place and God saying to you, *"whatever you set your eyes upon, I have given to you."* What made Abram a righteous man in the eyes of the Lord, was that he didn't just hear the word, but he believed God at His word and he acted on it.

There are many of us today who believe they have received a word from God, who are continuing to walk by faith and not by sight. May I encourage you today by saying, 'keep walking, keep believing, keep expecting, keep imagining!' Keep pulling what you are believing for towards you by using the power of your faith in God's word. Until you have what you are believing for, you have not come to the end of your faith. So, keep moving forward!

For the word of the Lord would say to you, this day-

> "Moreover, the Eternal One of Isra'el will not lie or change His mind, because He isn't a mere human being subject to changing His mind."
> -1 Samuel 15:29 (*ref:* Complete Jewish Bible)

And-

> "That by two unchangeable things, in which it is impossible for God to lie..."
> - Hebrews 6:18a

God's own words have revealed an absolute truth about Himself; He does NOT lie, and He does NOT change His mind. Don't allow yourself to become impatient and start looking at your own natural inabilities instead of the supernatural ability of God.

Eleven years have passed now and still Abram did not have an heir. Was it possible that he was beginning to focus on his own natural inability to produce an heir, that maybe he misunderstood God's plan when He said He would make him a great nation ($v.12:2$), that He would give his descendants all the land that was before him ($v.13:15$), and that his descendants would be as the dust of the earth ($v.13:16$)?

Could it be that God meant that one of his servants, born in his house, is who He was referring to as Abram's heir?

> But Abram said, "Lord God, what will You give me, seeing I go childless, and the heir of my house is Eliezer of Damascus?" Then Abram said, "Look, You have given me no offspring (seed); indeed, one born in my house is my heir!'
>
> -Genesis 15:2,3

I don't believe that Abram was asking God literally what He would give him, for God had been very clear as to what He would give to him. I don't believe Abram doubted that for a second.

What I believe he was questioning, was what God could give him that he could pass down from generation to generation seeing that he himself did not have an heir. You can almost get a sense of Abrams' anguish of wanting a son from his own loins and that it was quite possible he was becoming impatient and frustrated at God's words because even though promises were being made, Abram still did not have an heir to share it with.

I am sure there are times when we too would like for God to be a little bit more forth coming in His plan for how He will bring to pass what we are believing for.

> "And behold, the word of the Lord came to him, saying, 'This one shall not be you heir, but one who will come from your own body shall be your heir.'
>
> Then He brought him outside and said, 'Look, out towards heaven, and count the stars if you are able to number them.' And He said to him, 'So shall your descendants be.'"
>
> -Genesis 15:4,5

Now Abram receives some surety from the Lord that his heir *would* come from his own seed and not from a servant born in his house.

> "And he believed in the Lord, and He accounted it to him for righteousness."
>
> -Genesis 15:6

Abram did not have a faith problem, he might have had to deal with some impatience, possibly some frustrations in not seeing the whole picture but I do not believe it was a faith issue.

However, God still left out pertinent information in that He was not explicit with Abram from whom his heir would come. Why?

God must have known that by not telling Abram from whom his heir would come, that he and Sarai both would likely assume the child would come from someone else other than Sarai. Why?

And because God did not make this known straight away to him, or to Sarai, for that matter, it makes perfect since that Abram, knowing his wife was barren, would heed her request in making Hagar, her Egyptian maidservant, his wife and that she would conceive his heir (Gen.16:1-4).

Most sermons that talk about Abram, Sarai, and Hagar portray Abram as more than willing to go into Hagar's tent. She was depicted, after all, as a beautiful woman and what man would not go into another woman's tent at the consent of their wife?

I, however, do not believe this to be so. Sarai knew that God made Abram a promise, and in the natural, she knew she was barren and therefore, upon that belief system, knew she could not produce an heir and so she decided to take matters into her own hands.

> "So, Sarai said to Abram, 'see now, the Lord has restrained me from bearing children. <u>Please</u> go in to my maid; perhaps I shall obtain children by her;' And Abram heeded the voice of Sarai."
>
> -Genesis 16:2

I believe that Sarai gave her maidservant to Abram because she truly believed that God's covenant would naturally come through another woman. I believe this because the scripture says that she pleaded with him. I believe that Abram loved his wife with his whole heart and did not want to share a bed with another woman, regardless of her beauty. I believe that he too assumed it would be with someone other than Sarai because of her barrenness. And that is the only reason why He laid with Hagar.

This idea of course ended badly because Sarai began to despise Hagar for being pregnant and began to treat her with contempt. Because of Sarai's harsh treatment, Hagar runs away but an Angel of the Lord comes to her and tells her to return to Sarai and to submit herself under her mistress' hand.

The Lord then prophesies to Hagar; that she will have a son, his name shall be called Ishmael, and that her descendants would be multiplied exceedingly. Abram was eighty-six years old when Ishmael was born (Gen. 16:5-15).

This causes me to give pause here and ask, what was God thinking when He made the covenant with Abram but failed to tell him that this covenant would be through his wife, Sarai? If God knew Abram's heart concerning his wife, why wouldn't God stop him before He made the mistake of going into Hagar's bed? Finally, what was God's plan for Ishmael and his descendants'?

It wasn't until God appeared to him a second time, thirteen years later, that He established the covenant promise concerning his descendants. This time God comes to him in full transparency.

> "As for Me, behold, My covenant is with you, and you shall be a father of many nations.
>
> No longer shall your name be called Abram, but your name shall be Abraham; for I have made you a father of many nations (Strong's Concordance 1471: meaning foreign nations, Gentiles).
>
> I will make you exceedingly fruitful; and I will make nations of you, and kings shall come from you.
>
> And I will establish My covenant between Me and you and your descendants after you in their generations, for an everlasting covenant, to be God to you and your descendants after you."
>
> -Genesis 17:4-7

Abraham also had a part to play as well in this covenant: to see that every male child born among him, and his descendants would be circumcised on the eighth day as an outward sign of the covenant made between him and God.

Then God delivers a surprise that Abraham did not expect.... God tells him that his covenant is not with Ishmael, Hagar's son, but it will be with Sarai.

> "Then God said to Abraham, 'As for Sarai your wife, you shall not call her name Sarai, but Sarah shall be her name.
>
> And I will bless her and give you a son by her; then

> I will bless her, and she shall be a mother of nations; kings of peoples shall be from her.'"
>
> -Genesis 17:15,16

Abraham, who is ninety-nine now, laughs at the thought of his own ability to conceive a child with Sarai, who is ninety, and puts his son Ishmael before God, but God assures him that His word will come to pass (*v*.17,18).

> "No, Sarah, you wife, shall bear you a son, and you shall call his name Isaac; I will establish My covenant with him for an ever-lasting covenant, and with his descendants after him."
>
> -Genesis 17:19

God does reassure Abraham that He will surely bless Ishmael and will make him fruitful and multiply him exceedingly but His covenant with him will be established through Isaac alone (*v*.20).

In God's perfect timing, He did for Sarah as He promised and she conceived a son, and they called him Isaac. And Abraham circumcised him on the eighth day, as was his covenant agreement (Gen. 21:1).

Sarah lived for twenty-seven more years and saw her son grow to become a strong man before she was laid to rest in the land of Canaan. Abraham eventually marries again and has four sons with a woman named Keturah; altogether Abraham had a total of six sons that were born to him (Gen. 25).

Twenty-five years ago, God told Abraham to get out of

his country, leave his friends behind, and forsake his family and inheritance. Through his obedience, God made good on His promises: Abraham's name was great throughout the land of Canaan, his descendants became a great nation, God blessed him, and He made him to be a blessing. But what Abraham desired most, more than anything, came to fruition the day his covenant son was born to him.

What promises were given to you? How long have you been waiting to see God's word come to fruition in your life? Have you forgotten about it, laid it aside, maybe even given up and walked away from the vision He implanted in your heart? If so, I hope this testimony of Abraham's life inspires you to repent, turn back around, and allow God to speak to your heart once more.

I once missed an opportunity to take over a small television studio; we had access to a local station on Saturdays, and we used the time to have various preachers and teachers come on the air and preach the gospel, who otherwise, would not have the opportunity. But because I wanted to do it my way, it slipped right through my fingers. Needless to say, I lost the opportunity. But God is faithful to forgive and extend an abundance of grace and mercy to those who are willing to see their wrong and learn from it. Two years later, because of my faithful obedience, I have a new thriving ministry here in Cartersville, Georgia.

Fast tracking forward- Isaac was betrothed to Rebekah, and they begot Esau and Jacob. Because of Jacob's willingness to go along with his mother's deceitful plan to trick Isaac into giving him Esau's blessing, Jacob left his family for fear of repercussions from Esau and traveled to Haran to his uncle Laban's land- Rebekah's brother.

There he fell deeply in love with his uncle's youngest daughter, Rachel, and agreed to work seven years for her betrothment. But when he completed the agreed time, Laban deceived him by putting his oldest daughter before him. This would seem impossible for Jacob to make such a grave mistake, but the culture, at the time, was for the bride to be heavily veiled until she entered the bridal chamber and so it is very probable that Jacob naturally assumed he was receiving Rachel as his bride. To be honest, I have no excuse for him.

No one is sure how he could have made such a faux pas by consummating with the wrong bride. Some sages speculate that Laban might have encouraged him to drink too much before he went to her in hopes that he wouldn't notice that it was Leah. Perhaps because it was evening, he couldn't see her clearly enough, or just maybe, the two looked very similar to one another. Either way, the damage was done, Jacob was legally betrothed to Leah by morning. I don't think anyone thinks about Rachel, who I'm sure was under strict orders to stay in her room, knowing that her sister was going to marry the one that was meant for her.

To say the least, Jacob must have been livid with her father, whose only excuse was that their culture demanded that the eldest daughter marry first; nothing like leaving out pertinent information. However, I do not believe that Laban was ruled by his culture or the traditions of his fathers. I believe it stemmed from pure selfishness, knowing that if Jacob was with him, he would prosper.

However, Jacob would not wait for seven more years to go by before taking Rachel as his bride. He planned to receive her unto himself at once after his wedding week was over with Leah. Many believe that Jacob waited another seven years. But the scriptures say otherwise.

> "And Laban said, 'it must not be done so in our country, to give the younger before the firstborn. Fulfill her week (stay in the Bridal Chamber for the seven days as is required), and we will give you this one also for the service which you will serve with me still another seven years.'
>
> Then Jacob did so and fulfilled her week. So, he gave him his daughter Rachel as wife also."
> -Genesis 29:27,28

This might appear harsh, that Jacob would make Rebekah his wife directly after spending his wedding week with Leah, but there is no way that Leah was not as deceitful as her father in going along with his plan to deceive Jacob. And so, Jacob remained another seven years, as promised, with his uncle who continued to prosper because Jacob was with him (Gen. 29).

Over the years, Leah gave Jacob 4 sons: Rueben, Simeon, Levi, and Judah. When Rachel could not bear Jacob any children, she gave him her maidservant, Bil'hah who bore him 2 sons: Dan and Naphtali. When Leah stopped bearing children, she gave Jacob her maidservant, Zilpah, and she bore him 2 sons: Gad and Asher. Years later, Leah had 2 more sons: Issachar and Zebulun.

For years Rachel had been crying out to God for children and He heard her cries and opened her womb in which she gave Jacob his last two sons: Joseph and Benjamin. It was from those twelve sons that a nation was born to God: Israel.

In Genesis 35 we read that Jacob, whom God changed his name to Israel, took his family of 70 members, to Egypt to avoid the severe drought in the land they currently occupied.

For 430 years, Israel lived in the land of Goshen (Ex.12:40), and they became fruitful and multiplied. However, after Joseph died, there arose a Pharaoh who did not know him or the promises made to his family by the preceding Pharoah and began to fear the Israelites because their numbers exceeded the Egyptians (*Ex. 1:8, 9*). This new Pharaoh set taskmasters over them, forcing them into hard labor (*v.*10-14).

As a result, God's people were severely oppressed and began to cry out to God for their deliverance. When God heard their cries, He remembered His covenant to Abraham and began to set in motion their Exodus. Now we all know the story: God delivers Israel out of the hand of Pharaoh through the leading of Moses. Three months into the wilderness, He establishes a new covenant with the young nation.

This new covenant was not like the everlasting covenant He made with Abraham, Isaac, and Jacob, but one that was contingent on Israel keeping her promises to Him; that **if** they will obey His voice and keep His covenant terms and conditions, they would forever be a special treasure to Him above all people, a kingdom of priests, a holy nation (Ex.19:5-8).

The people agreed to hear this new covenant and so God gave Moses the Covenant of Laws and was instructed to read the terms and conditions out to the people in its entirety so that they would have full understanding of what it would mean for them to be under this covenant promise (*Ex. 24*). The people listened and agreed to all that was spoken that day.

> "And Moses took the blood and sprinkled it on the people, and said, 'This is the blood of the covenant which the Lord has made with you according to all these words.'"
>
> -Exodus 24:8

By agreeing to the covenant, God became a Husband to Israel.

> "...As in the days of her (Israel) youth, as in the day when she came up from the land of Egypt.
>
> And it shall be, in that day, Says the Lord, That you will call me 'My Husband,' and no longer call Me 'My Master'"
>
> -Hosea 2:15b,16

I would love to say that they lived happily ever after but unfortunately, as stories go, they didn't.

In 1 & 2 Kings and 1 & 2 Chronicles (*parts of the Ketuvim*

in the Tanakh) tells a vivid story of how Israel went on tumultuous roller coaster rides of twists and turns in their journey with God. Almost right out of the gate, Israel was not keeping the laws, statutes, and commandments that God set before them and soon began to violate their covenant promise to Him. We will look at that in the next chapter.

"For your Husband is your maker, whose name is the Lord of host; and your Redeemer is the Holy One of Israel, Who is called the God of all the earth. For a mere moment, I have forsaken you, but with great mercies I will gather you. With a little wrath I hid My face from you for moment (400 yrs.) but with everlasting kindness I will have mercy on you,"
says the Lord your Redeemer."

-Isaiah 54:5, 7,8

A Marriage Covenant of Laws- Broken

In Deuteronomy 7, God gives us a glimpse of how He has faithfully expressed His love towards Israel-

> "For you are a holy people to the Lord your God; the Lord your God has chosen you to be a people for Himself, a special treasure above all the peoples on the face of the earth.
>
> The Lord did not set His love on you nor choose you because you were more in number than any other people, for you were the least of all peoples;
>
> but because the Lord loves you, and because He would keep the oath which He swore to your fathers, ..."
>
> -Deuteronomy 7:6-8a

If you read Deuteronomy, chapters seven & eight, which I hope you do, you will begin to see how devoted He was to her:

- The assurance of His covenant promises and mercy towards her for a thousand generations.

- The bestowment of blessings that are assured to her for her faithfulness.

- His commitment to keep her safe from sickness and disease as they had once experienced in Egypt.

- Possession of the land that was promised to their fathers Abraham, Isaac, and Jacob.

- His enduring promise to protect and guard her against her enemies.

These are just a few of the promises that God affirmed over the people if they continued to keep themselves separate from their enemies, lest they fall to their own destruction.

In the beginning, Israel does start out as a loving wife towards her Husband, but unfortunately, it did not take long before she began to look upon other nations and see that they all had a king to judge over them. And so, they too desired to have a king to rule and reign over them as well.

This greatly displeased the prophet Samuel, who prayed to the Lord. "And the Lord said to Samuel-

> 'Heed the voice of the people in all that they say to you; for they have not rejected you, but they have rejected Me, that I should not reign over them.....'
>
> -1 Samuel 8:7

God heard their complaints and spoke to Israel through the prophet Samuel, forewarning them concerning the behavior of their chosen king and any future kings who would follow thereafter to rule and reign over them. Even when it was told to them that they would one day cry out to Him, He would not hear them.

> "and you will cry out in that day because of your king whom you have chosen for yourselves, and the Lord will not hear you in that day.
>
> Nevertheless, the people refused to obey the voice of Samuel; and they said, 'No but we will have a king over us,
>
> that we also may be like all the nations, and that our king may judge us and go out before us and fight our battles.'"
>
> -1 Samuel 8:18-20

To their own detriment, God heeded their voice and gave them a king.......Saul.

And as God had foreseen it, so did it come to pass- Saul took sons from their families and made them to plow his own land and reap his harvest; some would be made to make his weaponry and chariots; He took their daughters to be perfumers, cooks and bakers; He took their male and female servants and put them to work; and he took the best of the fields, olive groves, and vineyards for himself. These are just some of the things in which King Saul did before the people (1 Samuel 8).

Saul had only been king for two short years when he greatly sinned against God by performing a sacrifice that can only be done by a Levitical priest. The consequences for this careless and unholy act resulted in the loss of his kingship over the people of Israel.

I know this must seem a bit harsh, but Saul broke the Law of Moses by performing an unlawful sacrifice which was clearly done because of his impatience and disobedient pride. (*ref:* 1 Samuel 13 specifically verses 13,14)

Though Saul was king for many years thereafter, he knew God was no longer with him and it would be just a matter of time when God would raise up a successor; this time God will choose a king for Himself to rule over His people. As we know, He chose David.

Again, I would love to say that all was well within the kingdom of Jerusalem, but sadly no. David was not a perfect man, but he was always quick to repent when confronted with sin and had always accepted the consequences of his actions.

He had a heart to please God and constantly sought His face before making major decisions concerning the people. This is what made him a man after God's own heart; he walked before the Lord in truth and in righteousness for He loved the Lord with all his heart, all his mind, and with all his strength and for that, God had shown Him great mercy during his life. At the end of his reign, David named Solomon, whose mother was Bathsheba, as his successor.

For most of Solomon's life he followed God's ways, obeying His statutes and commandments as his father David did before him. But Solomon had a weakness for women specifically for beautiful foreign women. So much so, that at the end of his life, he had obtained seven hundred wives and three hundred concubines, all from various nations. Solomon knew that taking a wife or concubine from other nations was strictly against the law (Deut. 7:3,4).

Over time, his insatiable lust for women overcame him and his heart turned against the Lord. He built many places of worship to appease his wives desire to worship other gods and by doing this; he too began worshipping other gods just to please them. With great sin comes great consequences and though Solomon himself did not suffer these consequences; his actions affected all of Israel.

"Therefore, the Lord said to Solomon, 'Because you have done this, and have not kept My covenant and My statures, which I have commanded you, I will surely tear the kingdom away from you and give it to your servant (*Jeroboam*).

Nevertheless, I will not do it in your days, for the sake of your father David; I will tear it out of the hand of your son (*Rehoboam*).

However, I will not tear away the whole kingdom; I will give one tribe to your son for the sake of My servant David, and for the sake of Jerusalem which I have chosen.'"

-1 Kings 11:11-13

When Solomon died and his son, Rehoboam took the throne. It was not long before there was a revolt against Rehoboam and Israel was split into two nations as it was before with his grandfather David.

All through Kings and Chronicles we read about those who have reigned over Israel and Judah and how the majority of those kings were far worse than the one who preceded them. Only a small handful of kings followed after God's heart.

This reign of kings continued until God's anger kindled against both Israel and Judah. In circa 589-587 BC, God pronounced judgement on the Israelites and allowed King Nebuchadnezzar, of Babylon, to take both nations into captivity. For seventy years, the people were exiled from their lands and no longer belonged to themselves but were considered captives of Babylon.

Now I'll tell you about the day God divorced Israel. It was during the time the people were held in captivity, told through the book of Ezekiel. In my opinion, there is not a better book or chapter to explain what happened to Israel than to read for yourself from the book of Ezekiel.

Ezekiel 16 is a somewhat a somber allegory of Israel growing up from being an abandoned baby from birth into a young woman whom God fell in love with and took as His betrothed wife. *(v.1-6)* He consummated with her by entering into a Covenant relationship (*through Moses*). He washed her clean of impurities and clothed her with provisions that she would be in want of nothing. (*v.7-14*)

But Israel turned into a promiscuous woman who became unfaithful in all her ways. She followed the ways of other nations, even to the point of building idols and sacrificing their children to it. Over time, she forgot all that her loving Husband had done for her when she was naked and laid waste in her youth. (*v.15-22*)

As if that wasn't enough, Israel thought herself to be superior to all other nations and her insatiable appetite for lewd behavior even shocked the Philistine women who were known for their crude and offensive behavior. (*v.23-29*)

> "Behold therefore, I stretched out My hand against you, diminished your allotment (*your share, allowance*) and gave you up to the will of those who hate you, the daughters of the Philistines, who were ashamed of your lewd behavior."
>
> -Ezekiel 16:27

God's anger continued to kindle against His wife Israel. She became a brazen harlot who preferred strangers instead of her beloved Husband. So, God charged her as a willing adulterous who continually solicited others to come to her and He had finally had enough!

Because it was Israel who broke covenant with her Husband, God handed her a certificate of divorce (*Deut. 24:1*) and gave her over to her multiple lovers. The consequences of her sinful actions would be severe. (*v.30-34*)

> "and I will judge you as women who break wedlock and shed blood or judged: I will bring blood upon you in fury and jealousy."
>
> -Ezekiel 16:38

In verses 39-41 God pronounced judgment on His harlot wife, Israel.

- I will also give you into their hand, and they shall throw down your shrines and break down your high places (*where you have pagan worship*).

- They shall also strip you of your possessions, leaving you with nothing.

- They shall stone you and kill you with the sword.

- They shall burn your homes and destroy your properties.

- And execute you in the sight of many.

However, even in God's anger and promise to deal with Israel's sins, we still see His loving-kindness and mercy towards her. He reminds her that though she was the one who broke covenant with Him, nevertheless, He will remember the covenant that He made with her in the days of her youth (*v.59-60*) See also: Isaiah 54:4-8

> "and I will <u>establish</u> an <u>everlasting</u> Covenant with you."

God also makes it very clear that His new Covenant that He will reestablish with Israel will also include those outside- nations who have been around longer than Israel and those nations who are younger than Israel. This new Covenant will include all nations. *(v.61)*

> "And I will establish My Covenant with you. Then you shall know that I am the Lord, ... When I provide you atonement for all you have done, says the Lord God." (*v. 62,63*- Please read in its entirety)

Did you catch that!? Let us read it one more time!

.... "when I provide you atonement for all you have done," says the Lord God. That my friends, is our heavenly Father talking about His beloved Son Jesus!

It is ever so clear that God *will* establish an everlasting covenant through His beloved Son Jesus Christ, which would not only include Israel but all nations of the world. See also: Jeremiah 31:31-34, Hosea 2:

We know that God betrothed Israel as his bride, but over time she became an adulterous woman (*playing the harlot w/other nations*). This caused God, to hand her a certificate of divorce and according to Deut. 24:1-4, the law states that He can never remarry her. Does that mean that all of Israel is forsaken? No! Because though Israel is no longer His bride, He NEVER forsook His covenant with Abraham.

> "And I will establish My covenant between Me and you and your descendants after you in their generations, for an everlasting covenant, to be God to you and your

descendants after you."

-Genesis 17:7

From the beginning of time, God created and set in motion a plan for a *New Covenant* that is unconditional, that can never be broken, and is extended to both Jew and Gentile, male and female, slave or free.

This shows the amazing mercy and grace of God towards His people that He brought forth from the seed of Abraham. Through His mercy, He forgave Israel, and it is through His grace that He became Israel's Shadchan by sending His only begotten Son **that whosoever believes in Him** shall not parish but have everlasting life and not only for their sake but for the sake of all nations. (see also- Gen 17:5, Rom. 4, Gal. 3).

"For God so loved the world that He gave His only begotten Son, that whoever believes in Him should not perish but have everlasting life".

-John 3:16

More About Our Shadchan

Matchmaker

As we have read in the previous chapter, God had repositioned Himself from being a Husband to Israel, to the position of a *Shadchan*- Matchmaker.

> "Behold, the days are coming, says the Lord, when I will make a new covenant with the house of Israel and with the house of Judah-
>
> not according to the covenant that I made with their fathers in the day that I took them by the hand to lead them out of the land of Egypt, My covenant which they broke, though **I was a husband** to them, says the Lord.
>
> But this is the covenant that I will make with the house of Israel after those days, says the Lord: I will put My law [of love] in their minds, and write it on

their hearts; and I will be their God and they shall be My people.

No more shall every man teach his neighbor, and every man his brother, saying, 'Know the Lord', for they all shall know Me, from the least of them to the greatest of them, says the Lord. For I will forgive their iniquity, and their sin I will remember no more."
-Jeremiah 31:31-34

This promise was not only given to Israel but to all nations of the world, according to an everlasting covenant He made with Abraham.

> "For God said to Abraham, 'As for Me, behold, My Covenant is with you, and you shall be a father to many nations.'"
>
> -Genesis 17:4

God took one man, a Gentile, from his native land Ur, and birthed a nation. It is through this nation, Israel, that our Savior came, to whom also pertain the everlasting covenant, and to which the eternal promise of God extends to every Gentile who believes.

> "In past generations it was not made known to mankind, as the Spirit is now revealing it to His emissaries (*apostles*) and prophets;
>
> that in union with the Messiah and through the Good News the Gentiles were to be joint heirs, a joint body, and joint sharers with the Jews in what God has promised."

-Ephesians 3:5,6 (Complete Jewish Bible- cjb)

Gentiles were *never* a second thought to God; We were not a consolation prize because of Israel's rejection of Him. We were always at the forefront of His mind. It was God's perfect love that set-in motion a plan that would bring both Jews and Gentiles together in one body, through the cross. A love that would require Him to sacrifice His own beloved Son that we may have eternal life with Him.

> "And that He might reconcile them both to God in one body through the cross, thereby putting to death the enmity.
>
> And He came and preached peace to you [Gentiles] who were afar off and to those [Jews] who were near.
>
> For through Him we both [Jews and Gentiles] have access by one Spirit to the Father."
> -Ephesians 2:16-18

In the New Testament God is referred to as a Father over 250 times. The Greek word for father is "*pater*" (3962 Strongs Concordance) and it can mean: *a parent, a nourisher, or a protector.*

God no longer calls Himself a Husband to Israel, but rather He repositions Himself as a Shadchan to all nations who would call on the name of His beloved Son.

> "But as many as received [Jesus], to them He (*God*) gave the right to become children of God, to those

> who believed in His [Son's] name:
> who were born, not of blood, nor of the will of the flesh, nor of the will of man, but of God."
> -John 1:12,13

The Moody Bible Commentary explains it best- "becoming a child of God results in a spiritual "birth" produced by God's Spirit. Unlike human birth, Spiritual birth is not of blood, it is not the result of human descent. Neither is it of the will of the flesh, as if human desires can bring it about. Nor is spiritual birth of the will of man, negating any pride of males in producing children as was common in Jewish and other cultures. Contrary to anything innate, spiritual birth is an act of God"
(The Moody Bible Commentary, pg. 1608)

Before the foundation of the world ever existed, before He uttered the words, "let there be light," He chose *you*! He created *you* as a perfect match to His beloved Son, and in doing so, became a Father to *you*. He has known *you* and has loved *you* since the day He wove you in your mother's womb.

> "For You fashioned my inmost being, You knit me together **in my mother's womb**. I thank you because I am awesomely made wonderfully; Your works are wonders- I know this very well.
> -Psalm 139:13,14 (Complete Jewish Bible)

He put His Holy Spirit in *you* as a seal; a signet, that all would know who *you* are and to whom *you* belong.

> "In Him (Jesus) you also trusted; after you heard

> the word of truth, the gospel of your salvation;
> in whom also, having believed, **you were sealed
> with the Holy Spirit** of promise,"
>
> -Ephesians 1:13

It is His Holy Spirit who is *your* hope and guarantee that His Son will return for His beloved bride.

> [The Holy Spirit] "who is **the guarantee** of our inheritance [of eternal life] until the redemption of the purchased possession, to the praise of His glory."
>
> -Ephesians 1:14

And it is the fullness, the totality, and the divinity of His very being who resides in *your* heart continually!

> "For in Him <u>dwells</u> (*inhabits*) **all the fullness** of the Godhead bodily; and ***you* are <u>complete</u> in Him**, who is the head of all principality and power."
>
> -Colossians 2:9

This word, "complete" (4137 pleroo, Strongs Concordance) means: *to be to be full, crammed, jammed packed, or stuffed full*. Think about this- All that He is resides in *you*!

He has chosen *you* as His own child, setting *you* apart by His Spirit. And just as our Bridegroom gave gifts to us, His bride, our Heavenly Father has not come empty handed, for He too has bestowed gifts upon His children.

> "If you then, being evil [by nature], know how to give good gifts to your [own] children, how much more will **your Father** who is in heaven **give good things to those who ask Him**!"
> -Matthew 7:11

Let's take a look at just a few of those gifts-

The Gift of Eternal Life

> "For God so loved the world (*humankind*) that He gave [in betrothment] His only begotten Son, that whosoever believes in Him should not perish but have everlasting life.
>
> For God did not send His Son into [the midst of humankind] to condemn them but that they, through Him, might be saved."
> -John 3:16,17   (emphasis given for more clarity)

Jesus says- "I am the way, the truth, and the life. No one comes to the Father except through Me" (John 14:6). God's gift of eternal life can only be through His Son, Jesus Christ. It is by His shed blood that we have the forgiveness of sins, and it is by His sacrificed life that we are given eternal life.

The Gift of His Grace

> "For by grace, you have been saved through faith, and that not of yourselves; it is the gift of God."
> -Ephesians 2:8

Not only is the immeasurable gift of God's grace made available to us, but the capacity and capability to

The Gift of Adoption

> "just as He chose us in Him (*God*) before the foundation of the world, that we should be holy and without blame before Him in love,
>
> having predestined us to **adoption as <u>sons</u>** (a place of position, not about gender) by Jesus Christ to Himself, according to the good pleasure of His will."
> -Ephesians 1:4,5

In the Old Testament, there is no mention of the word "adoption". However, if you go back to Hosea 2:19-20 where the Lord is proclaiming Israel and Gentiles as both belonging to Him equally, you will see the word "betroth" written three times. This Hebrew word is "aras" (781 Strongs Concordance) and it means *-to engage in matrimony-* and it can also mean *-to adopt-*.

In his letter to the Ephesians (1:4,5), Paul states that before the foundation of the world was ever spoken into existence, God had already made up His mind about you. He saw your past, has looked into your future, and without hesitation chose you to be His child through the process of divine adoption.

The very moment we accepted Jesus into our hearts we went through a supernatural birthing process. We are born again, a new creation; old things have passed away; behold, all things have become new, through Christ.

Also-

Paul's letter to the Galatians gives us more elaborate details concerning our divine adoption.

> "But when the fullness of the time (*Gods timetable*) had come, God sent forth His Son, born of a woman, born under the law,
>
> to **redeem** those [Jews] who were under the law, that we [Jews] might receive the **adoption as sons.**
>
> And because you [Gentiles] are sons [through the seed of Abraham], God has set forth the Spirit of His Son into your hearts, crying out, "Abba Father!"
>
> Therefore, you are no longer a slave but a *son*, and if a *son*, then an heir of God."
>
> -Galatian 4:4-7

This is one of those Shelah moments. The word "redeem", is the Greek work "exagorazo" (59 Strongs Concordance), and it is specific to going to the marketplace to purchase a slave for the sole purpose of obtaining their freedom.

Jesus did not purchase our freedom just to put us under the slavery of the law. We are our Fathers children, but it is through Jesus' redemptive price, that we all take the position in His kingdom as sons

There's more-

The word "adoption as sons" is one word, "huiothesia" (5206 Strongs Concordance), and it can mean: *the placing of a son, or sonship*. It is important to note, especially if you are female, that this word is not specific to any one gender but rather a place of position: Jesus being the firstborn over all creation (Col. 1:15).

What Paul is conveying here is equality amongst all God's children, having been raised to the status of sonship with rights and privileges equal to a firstborn son. This again, has nothing to do with gender and everything to do with position.

Regardless of whether you are male or female, Jew or Greek, if you believe in your heart and have confessed with your mouth that Jesus is Lord, you have been raised to the position of sonship; no one can take this away from you!!!!

> "For you are all <u>sons</u> (*children*) of God through faith in Christ Jesus.
>
> For as many of you as were [spiritually] baptized into Christ have put on Christ.
> There is neither Jew nor Greek, there is neither slave nor free, there is neither male nor female; for you are *all* one in Christ Jesus.
>
> And if you are Christ's, then you are Abraham's seed, and heirs according to the promise."
> -Galatians 3:26-29

This means that we are His heir, all that He has, we have access to.

> "For as many as are led by the Spirit of God, these are sons of God.

> For you did not receive the spirit of bondage again to fear, but you received the Spirit of adoption by whom we cry out, "Abba Father.
>
> The Spirit Himself bears witness with our spirit that we are children of God,
>
> and if children, then heirs of God, and joint heirs with Christ,..."
> -Romans 8:14-17a (*read the scriptures in its entirely*)

There's more-
Paul reveals God's heart towards us as a Father in that we are given the privilege of calling Him, "Abba". He mentions this also in his letter to the Romans.

> "For you did not receive the spirit of bondage again to fear, but you received the spirit of adoption by whom we cry out, "**Abba Father**."
>
> -Romans 8:15

In a Jewish home, only a child who has been born to the patriarch of that household has the right to call him 'Abba'. It is not permitted for a servant who was bought or raised under the same household to call the patriarch, Abba. Both Jews and Gentiles alike have the right and privilege of calling Him Father.

We are not to walk around as if we are His stepchildren or His servants, hoping He will listen to our prayers. Think about this- we are, more closely related with one another by the blood of Jesus, that flows through our veins, then we are through our own blood relatives.

> "Not only that, but we also who have the first fruits of the Spirit, even we ourselves groan within ourselves, eagerly waiting for the adoption, the redemption of our body."
>
> -Romans 8:23

Growing up, I have had a few stepfathers, none of which took the time to sow into my life. When I received Jesus into my heart, I did not know that I would be receiving an amazing gift of sonship with all the rights and privileges of a first-born heir.

Through adoption, God has set in order a bond that can NEVER be broken, nor can we EVER be separated from His presence.

> "I give them eternal life, and they shall never perish; **neither shall anyone snatch them out of My hand**.
>
> My Father, who has given them to Me, is greater than all; and no one is able to snatch them out of My Father's hand. My Father and I are one."
>
> -John 10:28,29

Lastly, think about this: there are well over 900 names, titles, and attributes that describe the very nature of who He is. And yet, of all those, He desires to draw near to us as a loving Father.

To me, He is my Dad!

"Then He took the cup, and when He had given thanks, He gave it to them, and they all drank from it. And He said to them, "This is My blood of the new covenant which is shed for many."

-Mark 14:23,24

More About The Cup

Sefel

All four Gospels give an account of Jesus' last night with His disciples. Although each one has their own personal recounting of what happened up to the time of His death, we are unable to see the full picture with just one perspective. We need all four viewpoints to unveil more clearly what took place that Passover night.

With that said, I would encourage you to study all four accounts. For this chapter, I will, for the most part, be using Luke's account.

The Night of Passover

> "Then came the Day of Unleavened Bread when Passover must be <u>killed</u> (*sacrificed*).
>
> And He sent Peter and John, saying, 'Go and prepare

the Passover for us, that we may eat.'"

-Luke 22:7,8

At this point, Judas Iscariot had already approached the chief priests asking for a reward if he agreed to turn Jesus over to them. They immediately paid him thirty pieces of silver. (Mat. 26:15,16)

"When the hour had come, He sat down, and the twelve apostles with Him.

Then He said to them, 'With desire I have desired to eat this Passover with you before I suffer;

for I say to you, I will no longer eat of it until it is fulfilled in the kingdom of God.'"

-Luke 22:14-16

For a little over three years, all twelve disciples have sat under Jesus' teachings. Now these disciples, less one (Judas), have graduated to Apostleship; messengers commissioned to preach the gospel under the direction of His Holy Spirit.

The word "desire" tells us that Jesus had set his heart on this last Passover, that He longed with great zeal to celebrate it with the ones He spent so much time with. For Him, the anticipation of finishing what He had come to do overshadowed the anguish and pain that was soon to follow. He would not celebrate another Passover for He Himself was to be God's sacrificed Passover Lamb- John 1:29.

The Bride's Cup-

I believe that Jesus and His disciples finished the Passover meal together, and it was after the meal was finished, did He then institute the <u>new Covenant</u> (Communion), not during.

> "Then He took the cup (*sefel*), and gave thanks, and said, 'Take this and divide it among yourselves;
>
> for I say to you, I will not drink of the fruit of the vine until the kingdom of God comes.'
>
> And He took bread, gave thanks, and broke it, and gave it to them, saying, 'This is My body which is given for you; do this in remembrance of Me.'
>
> Likewise, He also took the [same] cup **after supper**, saying, 'This cup is the new covenant in My blood, which is shed for you.'"
>
> -Luke 22:17-20

John does not mention the Passover meal nor the <u>new covenant</u> (*communion*). However, Matthew and Mark's account is almost verbatim of each other, and only give a short synopsis of that night. I believe that Luke and Paul's account is more accurate. Let's read Paul's account, from the Lord Himself.

> "For I (*Paul*) received from the Lord that which I also delivered to you: that the Lord Jesus on the same

night in which He was betrayed took bread;

and when He had given thanks, He broke it and said, 'Take, eat; this is my body which is broken for you; do this in remembrance of Me.'

In the same manner He also took <u>the cup after supper</u>, saying, 'This cup is the new covenant in My blood. This do, as often as you drink it, in remembrance of Me.'"

-1 Corinthians 11:23-25

After reading all four accounts, I believe that it was only when they had eaten their Passover meal and had their fill of the new wine that Jesus lifted up *one* cup, gave thanks, and gave it to them to divide amongst themselves into their own individual cup. He also took bread, representing His body, gave thanks, and broke it, giving it to them in which they partook of.

Likewise (*in the same manner*), He lifted that same cup that He had just instructed them to divide amongst themselves and told them to drink, for it is the covenant of His blood being shed for them (and us).

Now if we were to follow the ancient traditions of both bride and bridegroom sharing a cup of wine, we would have to find out *when* Jesus accepted His cup because He did not partake of the same cup as the disciples nor did he eat the bread that represented His own body. Jesus would not have drunk from a cup that would symbolize His own blood, and He wouldn't have eaten bread that represented His own body.

This cup that He offered to His disciples and offers to us today is for us alone, the bride, to take in remembrance of the blood He shed for us on the cross. That leaves us with a very important question of when did our Bridegroom partake of His portion of the cup that would betroth us to Himself?!

Our Bridegrooms Cup-

Tradition says that unless the bridegroom partakes of the cup, they are not betrothed to one another. Jesus must receive His portion before He leaves this earth to go to His Father's house, otherwise His betrothment to us would be null and void.

Following Him to the Garden of Gethsemane, Jesus asks the Father if there was any way this cup could pass.

> ".....O My Father, if it is possible, let this cup pass from Me;......

Not that He wasn't willing, but I believe Jesus was searching through time, the end from the beginning, to see if this betrothment could be done by any other means. Seeing that it could not, He responded as any bridegroom would who so deeply loved their bride and desired to be with her.

> Nevertheless, not as I will, but as You will."
> -Matthew 26:39

> "And again, a little while longer, He prayed,

> saying, 'O My Father, if this cup cannot pass away from Me unless I drink it, Your will be done.'"
> -Matthew 26:42

> "He went away again, and prayed the third time, saying the same words."
> -Matthew 26:44

At this point Jesus still has not taken His portion from the cup that would betroth His bride to Himself. The only place this could have been done was when He was on the cross!

> "After this, Jesus, knowing that all things were now accomplished, that the Scripture might be fulfilled, said, 'I thirst!'"
>
> Now a vessel full of sour wine was sitting there; and they filled a sponge with sour wine, put it on hyssop, and put it in His mouth.
>
> So, when Jesus had received the sour wine, He said, 'It is finished!' And bowing His head, He gave up His Spirit. "
> -John 19:28-30

Jesus would not have left this earth without taking His portion of the cup. That can only leave one other opportunity before He gave up His Spirit and left this earth: the cross!

I have heard these two words, "I thirst," be interpreted as Jesus being thirsty for His people, but no sermon could possibly give any other explanation other than He was fulfilling the prophecy that would betroth Himself to His bride: YOU.

Most will tell you that getting baptized is vital to a new believer's salvation. And though it is something that should be done as soon as possible, I believe that taking communion, as the bride of Christ, should be a priority. If you disagree, "just spit the bones out," as a good friend once said to me.

"I indeed baptize you with water unto repentance, but He who is coming after me is mightier than I, whose sandals I am not worthy to carry, He will baptize you with the Holy Spirit."

-Matthew 3:11

More About The Mikvah

Baptism

Let me start off making a bold statement by saying, "Baptism is NOT a salvation issue." There are certain denominations, commentators, and lay persons who believe in baptismal regeneration: that baptism is essential for salvation and that without the baptism of water, one cannot be saved or born again. However, there are no foundational truths to this belief. Being baptized in and of itself does not wash your sins away, nor does it bring salvation. Only by one's confession that Jesus Christ is Lord, can one be saved.

> "that **if** you **confess with your mouth** the Lord Jesus and **believe in your heart** that God has raised Him from the dead, you will be saved.
>
> For with the heart one believes unto righteousness, and with the mouth confession is made unto salvation."

-Romans 10:9,10

If Paul was going to make it clear on the subject of salvation through baptism, he would have added.... *"and be baptized in water"* in his letter to the people who were hearing the message.

In fact, in verse 13, Paul reiterates this truth by quoting a portion of an Old Testament verse in the book of Joel.

> "And it shall come to pass that whoever calls on the name of the Lord shall be <u>saved</u> (*delivered*).."
> -Joel 2:32a

Now let's take a quick look back in history and see what we can find-

Old Testament-

Baptisms are not mentioned under the ceremonial laws of Moses. However, certain instances did require various washings in water for the purpose of purification as briefly mentioned in Hebrew 9:10. Some ceremonial washings would include, but I'm sure not limited to....

Priests washing their hands and feet in the bronze laver before entering the Tabernacle in their daily services, or when they came near the altar to minister burnt offerings unto the Lord. This purification washing was done for their own protection *"lest they die"* (Ex. 30:17-24).

- The High Priest, on the Day of Atonement (after he had made atonement for himself, his family,

and the assembly of the people) would enter the tabernacle of meeting, remove his linen garments, and *"wash his body"* (Leviticus 16:17-24).

- The one who released the goat as the scapegoat was required to wash his clothes and bathe his body in water before he could come back into camp. And the one who was responsible for burning the carcasses of the bull and the sacrificial goat outside of camp, was also required to wash their clothes and bathe their body before coming back into the camp (Lev. 16:26-28).

- In preparation of religious festivals (Ex. 19:10 & John 11:55).

Other occasions found in the Old Testament:
- Having to wash their clothes if they have come in contact with a dead animal or corpse (Lev. 11).

- A leper who has been cleansed of leprosy (Lev. 14:8).

- See also Leviticus 15 concerning men and women becoming unclean and needing to wash themselves.

These are just a few instances where we can clearly see the importance of various types of washings and the health benefits thereof. However, nowhere in the Old Testament, that I could find, was there an ordinance that required a physical baptism (*fully submersed in water*) for the purpose of being purified, declared holy, and set apart for God.

John the Baptist

John's ministry of water baptism was focused on getting the people prepared for their coming Messiah through repentance, the confession of sins.

> *v.*4 "John came baptizing in the wilderness and preaching a baptism of repentance for the remission of sins."
>
> *v.*7 "and he preached, saying, 'There comes One after me who's mightier than I, whose sandal strap I am not worthy to stoop down and loose.
>
> *v.*8 'I indeed <u>baptize</u> (*immerse*) you with water, but He will <u>baptize</u> (*immerse*) you with the Holy Spirit.'"
> -Mark 1: 4,7,8

The Gospels do not testify whether or not the ones coming to be baptized were Jews or Gentiles, but the Jewish people would have clearly understood what John the Baptist was calling for: a repentant heart towards God. Little did they know that they would soon be meeting Him face to face.

Also notice that John does not say that Jesus will baptize them with water but with the Holy Spirit. Matthew and Luke also record the same statement.

> "John answered, saying to all, 'I indeed baptize you with water; but One mightier than I is coming whose sandal strap I am not worthy to loosen. He will baptize you with the Holy Spirit and fire.'"

-Luke 3:16

"I indeed baptize you with water unto repentance, but He who is coming after me is mightier than I, whose sandals I am not worthy to carry. He will baptize you with the Holy Spirit and fire'"

-Matthew 3:11

The Early Church

Before Jesus ascended, He instructed His eleven disciples-

> 'All authority has been given to Me in heaven and on earth.
>
> Go therefore and make disciples of <u>all the nations, baptizing them</u> in the name of the Father and the Son and of the Holy Spirit,
>
> teaching them to observe all things that I have commanded you; and lo, I am with you always, even to the end of the age.'" Amen.

-Matthew 28:18b-20

In the early church, it was expected that directly after one received Jesus by confession, they would immediately be baptized in a public setting.

But it is only in the name of Jesus by which we are saved! And whose name alone gives us the forgiveness of sins, NOT in the act of baptism.

> "Then Peter said to them, 'Repent, and let every one of you be baptized **IN** <u>the name of Jesus Christ</u>

> for the <u>remission</u> (*forgiveness*) of sins; and you shall receive the Holy Spirit.'"
>
> -Acts 2:38

I believe that baptism was essential during the early church period, both for the Jews and for the Gentiles. For the Jews, it signified their acknowledgement and acceptance that Jesus was, in fact, their Messiah. There were some who believed but because of their fear of being excommunicated from their Synagogue, they would not openly confess.

> "Nevertheless, even among the rulers many believed in Him. But because of the Pharisees they did not confess Him, lest they should be put out of the synagogue;
>
> for they loved the praise of men more than the praise of God.
>
> -John 12:42,43

Jesus made it very clear when He said-

> "Therefore whoever confesses Me before men, him I will also confess before My Father who is in heaven.
>
> But whoever denies Me before men. Him I will also deny before My Father who is in heaven."
>
> -Matthew 10:32,33

Peter didn't throw any punches when it came to the seriousness of one's faith in Jesus, even to the point of reminding them that it was by their own hand that Jesus was crucified, Acts 2.

For the Gentiles, it was equally imperative that they too be baptized. There were countless gods that were worshipped among the Romans, Greeks, and Egyptians at that time, and many of them were baptized in the name of their false gods.

Being baptized in the name of God the Father, God the Son, and God the Holy Spirit would have made an impact on their lives and shown to be an open witness to any member of the audience, that Jesus is the One true God, and only He is to be truly worshipped.

Baptism, in my opinion, is to be taken very seriously and celebrated; it is an open declaration of what you believe on the inside is made manifest on the outside and leaves no doubt to any onlookers in whom you believe.

Not only as an outward testament of one's faith but also as an open demonstration that we too are being identified with Him in His death and resurrection when we go through the ritual of baptism; for we have also died (*to our old ways*) and have been raised from the dead by the glory of God the Father.

> "Or do you not know that as many of us as were <u>baptized</u> (*fully immersed*) into Christ Jesus were <u>baptized</u> (*fully immersed*) into his death?
>
> Therefore, we were buried with Him through baptism into death, that just as Christ was raised from the dead by the glory of the Father, even so we also should walk in newness of life."

-Romans 6:3,4

Also-

> "For you are all <u>sons</u> (*a place of position*) of God through faith in Christ Jesus.
>
> For as many of you as were <u>baptized into Christ have put on Christ</u>.
>
> There is neither Jews nor <u>Greek</u> (*Gentile*), there is neither slave nor free, there is neither male nor female; for you are all one in Christ Jesus."
> -Galatians 3:26-28

This last scripture must be read carefully so that there is no room for misinterpretations. Paul says, "For as many of you as were baptized INTO Christ have PUT ON Christ."

The word, "*into*" indicates a specific point reached or a point of entry, which means that the moment we received His Holy Spirit, we have become one with Him.

The next half of Paul's statement says, "*have put on Christ.*" This gives a sense of sinking into a garment, to be clothed in Christ as in a new creation; old things have passed away behold all things have become new (2 Cor. 5:17).

Here are a few others to consider-

> ....."And such were some of you. But you were <u>washed</u>, (*cleansed from sin*) but you were <u>sanctified</u> (*separated from sin*), but you were <u>justified</u> (*made innocent*) in

the name of the Lord Jesus and by the Spirit of our God."

-1 Corinthians 6:11

Paul is talking about a spiritual washing that takes place when we receive Jesus. It is because we are Christians (followers of Christ) that we have been fully washed by the Spirit of God. Our debts have been canceled out automatically and without a conscious thought by our Lord and Savior, Jesus.

Here is another example of being washed in water.

> "Husbands, love your wives, just as Christ also loved the <u>church</u> (*His bride*) and gave Himself for her,
>
> that He might sanctify and cleanse her with the washing of water <u>by the word</u>"

-Ephesians 5:25,26

Again, we see this word, "*washing*" but the water spoken of is used figuratively as we cannot literally be washed in words, but we most certainly can undergo a spiritual washing in the word.

> The Moody Bible Commentary says- "Baptism does not save an individual, but it serves as the profound sign of the prior work of God who cleanses one from the corruption of sin at the time of salvation." (A one-volume commentary on the whole Bible by the faculty of Moody Bible Institute, pg. 1783).

So, does baptism have any significance in our Christian walk today? Absolutely! However, there are some scriptures that can be misinterpreted; making it appear that baptism is mandatory for salvation and though it has great signification, again it is not a salvation issue.

Jesus says-

> "Go into the world and preach the gospel to every creature.
>
> He who believes and is baptized will be saved; but he who <u>does not believe</u> will be <u>condemned</u> (*damned*)"
> -Mark. 16:15,16

The second half of this verse explains the first half. You can believe and be baptized (as an open declaration) and be saved. However, if you do not believe, it wouldn't matter if you were baptized or not, you will be condemned.

Jesus was making it very clear here, that it is by our faith in Him alone that saves us, and it is by our lack of faith that condemns us.

Baptism does not save you; it is simply an outward expression of what has already happened spiritually to your inward man. It is not the outward man that is cleansed from sin but the inward man.

In fact, I do not see anything wrong with getting baptized more than once. I have personally been baptized twice in my renewed life. I was baptized in a swimming pool a couple of years after I was born (again), and I was baptized in the Jordan River in Israel, what an experience!

"And Jesus cried out again with a loud voice and yielded up His Spirit. Then behold, the veil of the temple was torn in two from top to bottom. and the earth quaked, and the rocks were split."

-Matthew 27:50,51

The Veil

Of The Covering

In my research of betrothed women wearing veils, I have found that most "*experts on the matter*" only go as far back as the Roman and Greek era; the brides would wear veils of fiery reds and yellows for the purpose of warding off evil spirits. However, if you did not know about ancient Jewish culture, it would be easy to miss the fact that veils dated at least as far back as fifteen-hundred years; before Christ was born. In our Christian History Book, the Old Testament, it is recorded in Genesis 24 that Rebekah veils herself when she is told that Isaac, her betrothed, is approaching her caravan.

A betrothed bride was expected to wear her veil whenever she was in the presence of men who were outside of her immediate family. By this simple act, she is letting everyone know that she is no longer available for suitors, she has been bought for a price and belongs to another. Only when her betrothed removes the veil in their Bridal Chamber and their marriage consummated, would she then not be required to wear one outside the home.

Through the Centuries, the meaning of the wedding veil has changed; Christian women began wearing veils over their faces when they walked down the aisle to symbolize their purity and virginity. This tradition eventually became a common practice among all women in Western culture. However, by the time the Victorian era came into play, the veils became more of a status symbol; measured by the length, the weight of the fabric and how elaborately embellished it was pieced together.

Over the course of time, the true meaning of the veil had become lost amongst traditions of family and culture. Today, it is rare to see a bride wearing a veil that covers her face on her wedding day unless it is an accessory to her ensemble.

All over the world, there are many museums displaying exquisite veils with wedding dresses that queens and other famous women have worn with all the particulars as to who wore it and in what era.

However, I truly believe that the most elaborate veil ever made in the history of mankind, was the veil of the Tabernacle that God personally designed for His brides covering.

When reading the scriptures, it might seem that God had the veil made with the intention of keeping Himself hidden from the people of Israel. But in actuality, it was for Israels protection that God had the veil made; for no man can see Him and live.

> "And he (Moses) said, 'Please, show me Your glory.'
>
> Then He (*God*) said, 'I will make all My goodness pass before you, and I will proclaim the name of the Lord before you. I will be gracious to whom I will be gracious, and I will have compassion on whom I will have compassion.'
>
> But He said, 'you cannot see My face; for no man shall see Me and live'."
>
> -Exodus 33:18-20

God desired to be with His people. However, in order to do that, He would need to have a structure built that could inhabit His presence and make it safe for them to receive Him. This is why He had a tabernacle built to certain specifications that would house the very presence of His glory. As He told Moses.....

> "And there [in the Holy of Holies] **I will meet with you**, and I will speak with you from above the mercy seat, from between the two cherubim which *are* on the ark of the Testimony, about everything which I will give you in commandment to the children of Israel."
>
> -Exodus 25:22

If you have a desire to really visualize how the tabernacle

was pieced together, read Exodus Chapters 25-31 with 35-40. Otherwise, I will be happy to offer an overview.

The **Tabernacle of God** had two rooms: the sanctuary (also known as the holy place) and the Holy of Holies (or Most Holy Place). Within the structure, there were two veils: one veil was used as a door to separate the sanctuary from the outer courts and the second veil separated the Holy of Holies from the sanctuary.

The walls of the tabernacle measured fifteen feet high, fifteen feet wide, and forty-five feet long, and were constructed of acacia wood panels. The ceiling consisted of four distinct types of curtain coverings.
The first covering, which would have been the inner ceiling of the tabernacle, was made of fine linen of blue, purple, and scarlet threads, with designs of cherubim woven into the fabric. The second covering was of goats' hair; the third, ram skins dyed red; and the fourth and final covering was badger skins to prevent water from seeping in from the rains.

The structure was built in such a way that when assembled, there was not any natural light emitted into either room. The sanctuary was the only room of the two that was lit, and it received its light from the seven candles on the golden lampstand. Yet, inside the Holy of Holies, it was pitch black.

The **Tabernacle veil** which separated the inner sanctuary from the Holy of Holies must have been magnificent to behold; threads of blue, purple, and scarlet were woven into plaits with designs of Cherubim worked into the fabric and was pieced together exactly like the one that covered the ceiling. It hung as a single piece of material by gold hooks on a rod, interlaid with gold that extended the length of the doorway, measuring thirty feet wide, and thirty feet long. Though there are no specifics on its width, it would be easy to assume by the number of threads being used, the veil was extremely thick and heavy.

When I began to study about how the veil was pieced together, it was hard not to be so impassioned thinking about all the intricate details that must have gone into the work needed to construct and assemble the Tabernacle: the side panels, the ceiling covers, all the furnishings, and the Ark of the Covenant with the mercy seat.

I tried to imagine what it must have been like for that gifted artisan, who was supernaturally endowed by God, to create the ark and mercy seat where God Himself would rest. I tried to visualize him taking a cloth and giving it one more go-over before he walked out of the Holy of Holies, closing the veil behind him. Did he even realize that he would be the last human being who would ever touch the Ark of the Covenant and mercy seat of God?

As we finish reading about the completed construction of the tabernacle, we can only attempt to visualize how incredible this structure was when it was all said and done, and how meticulous God was in every aspect of its assembly.

If we completely understood why He had a covering built in such a way, we would come to the conclusion that though they (we) were created in His likeness, He is a Spirit, and we in our mere human state, are incapable of standing in the midst of the fulness of the brightness of His glory without a covering to safeguard us.

If He was going to be among His people, they had to follow strict guidelines for their own protection. And if we know anything about God, we know that He has a deep love that know no boundaries, and here we see a small glimpse of it as He attempts to fellowship with His people.

Getting back to the tabernacle, it was only the tribe of Levi who were allowed to attend to the needs of the tabernacle, by performing daily duties, and only the high priest was allowed to enter through the second veil (holy of holies), but once a year, and never without an offering of blood.

> "Now when these things had been thus prepared (the temple furniture), the priests always went into the <u>first part of the tabernacle</u> (*the sanctuary*), performing the services.
>
> But into the <u>second part</u> (*holy of holies*) the **high priest went in alone once a year, not without blood**, which he offered for himself and for the people's sins committed in ignorance, "
>
> -Hebrew 9:6,7

To enter in at ones choosing would mean certain death, for God Himself has said, "by those who come near Me, I *must* be regarded as holy; and before all the people, I *must* be glorified", Lev. 10:3. To not regard God as most holy was to their own detriment.

Before the Tabernacle was built, we read in the book of Exodus, how God always appeared to the people of Israel in a thick cloud covering so as not to be seen. Even at Moses' request to see His face, God could only show his backside to him less he perished, *"for no man can see God and live"*. By His very Presence among them, He could consume the people right where they stood, Ex. 33:18-23.

King **Solomon's Temple** was built on Mt. Moriah (circa mid-10th century), and all the furnishings that was in the tabernacle, including the two veils, were brought into this magnificent temple. It is recorded in 1 Kings 8:1-11 and 2 Chronicles 5, that 120 priests with musicians came together in the Temple singing praises of thanksgiving to the Lord for hours on end until they could no longer continue; for the shekinah glory cloud of the Lord filled the Temple and **His very presence prohibited them from remaining inside**.

Reading through the books of Samuel, Kings and Chronicles, we know that God did not always occupy the Tabernacle of Moses nor Solomon's Temple. Nonetheless, the holy place where the ark stood and the ark itself, with the mercy seat, was to be regarded as most holy.

History tells us that Solomon's Temple stood for 476 years until its utter destruction in 586BC, by King Nebuchadnezzar. It was just before the Babylonian invasion that God speaks to Jeremiah about taking the ark with the mercy seat, the veil, and the temple furnishings to

Mount Nebo and bury them in a cave. Coming back from his journey, when the priests ask him where he buried the ark, Jeremiah's reply was, "If God wants you to know where it is, He will tell you".   2 Maccabees 2:4-10.

To this day, these items have not been found! It would be approximately 400 years later before anyone would experience the presence of God again and certainly not like anyone would have imagined!

King **Herod's Temple** was a renovation of the second temple that was reconstructed by the Jews who came out of exile in 515BC. To put this into perspective of God's perfect timing in sending His Son, here are a few facts you may not have known was going on at the time of Jesus' ministry-

- The ark, with all the original temple furnishings, was still missing at the time of Jesus' ministry.

- The Levitical priesthood's bloodline was corrupted by their own immoral actions from generation to generation, Ezra 9.

- The Roman Emperor, Tiberius Julius Caesar Augustus, appointed the high priest, and it was well known that the position could be given through bribes and ones promise to control the Jewish community.

- The appointed high priest at the time was Caiaphas, a morally corrupt and vicious man.

- Along with his father-in-law, Annas, they were two of the most influential and corrupt men in all of Jerusalem and ruled the people through religious law.

- Most of the Sanhedrin council along with the legalistic Pharisees were corrupt and known to take bribes.

- The temple courts were being used as a marketplace for the selling of sacrificial animals.

Needless to say, the house of God was left desolate of His presence and had been for quite some time.

It would not be until the birth of His only begotten Son that God would once again be among His people, as was prophesied through the prophet Isaiah-

> "Therefore the Lord Himself will give you a sign: Behold, the virgin shall conceive and bear a Son, and shall call His name **Immanuel** [**God with us**]."
>
> -Isaiah 7:14

And came to pass through the virgin Mary-

> "And she (*Mary*) will bring forth a Son, and you (*Joseph, husband to Mary*) shall call His name JESUS, for He will save His people from their sins,
>
> So all this was done that it might be fulfilled which was spoken by the Lord through the prophet

[Isaiah], saying:

> "Behold, the virgin shall be with child, and bear a Son, and they shall call His name **Immanuel**," which is translated, "**God with us**."
>
> -Matthew 1:21-23

But this time He came housed in flesh and blood, and for three years He walked among the people and ministered to them but the world did not know Him; He came to His own people but they would not receive Him- John 1:10,11. And when He was innocently crucified, He yielded up His Spirit, and it was at that very moment that the veil between the Sanctuary and the Holy of Holies was torn from top to bottom.

> "And Jesus cried out again with a loud voice and yielded up His Spirit.
>
> Then behold, the **veil** of the temple was torn in two from top to bottom; and the earth quaked, and the rocks were split."
>
> -Matthew 27:50,51

With the veil being torn in such a way, in which it could not have been pieced back together, gave a clear and present sign that God has given us a new and living way to enter into His holy presence; through the freshly slain blood sacrifice of His beloved Son, Jesus Christ.

This mohar (_____) was not just for the Jews only but <u>for all nations</u> as was promised through God's Covenant with Abraham- Genesis 17:4.

> "For by grace you [Jew and Gentile] have been saved through [your] faith, and that not of yourselves (*volition*), **it is the gift of God."**
> -Ephesians 2:8

As Gentiles (*non-Jews*) we had no hope for we were outsiders from the beginning. In the letter to the Ephesians, Paul writes specifically concerning this very issue-

> "Therefore remember that you, once Gentiles in the flesh-
>
> .....were without Christ, being <u>aliens</u> (*outsiders*) from the <u>commonwealth of Israel</u> (*non-citizens*) and strangers from the <u>covenants of promise</u> (*the law,*) having no hope and without God in the world.
>
> But now **in Christ Jesus [Gods plan for you]**, you who once were far off, have been brought near by the blood (*the mohar*) of Christ."
> -Ephesians 2:11a, 12,13

Then Paul says something incredibly significant to the Gentiles-

> "For He Himself is our peace, who has made both (*Jews, Gentiles*) one, and has <u>broken down the middle wall</u> of separation,
>
> having abolished in His flesh the enmity, that

is, the law of commandments contained in
ordinances, so as to create in Himself one new
man from the two, thus making peace."
-Ephesians 2:14,15

The middle wall mentioned here in Ephesians 2:14, was a four-foot-high partition, with thirteen separate openings set equally apart around the wall. At each opening, there was a sign posted, written in Greek that states:
"No foreigner is to enter the barriers surrounding the sanctuary. He who is caught will have himself to blame for his death which will follow."
(biblehistory.net/wall_of_separation)

Only the Jewish community to pass through to the temple side. The Gentiles could only come so far and no further.

By our Bridegroom's priceless sacrifice, both Jews and Gentiles have become the very Temple of God!!

- And as a living stone, **we are** being built up as a spiritual house, a holy priesthood, that we may offer up spiritual sacrifices of praise and thanksgiving, acceptable to Him through His beloved Son, Jesus Christ (1 Pt. 2:4,5).

- **We are** no longer strangers and foreigners (*sojourners*), but fellow citizens with the saints and fellow members of the household of God (Eph. 2:19).

- Even now, **we are** being fitted together, growing

into a holy temple in the Lord, being built together for a dwelling place of God in the Spirit (Eph. 2:21,22).

- **We are** the ark of the new Covenant, where the presence of His Shekinah glory resides. Our bodies are the Temple of His Holy Spirit who is in you, whom you have from God. You are no longer your own for you have been bought at a price; therefore, we have a responsibility to glorify God in our bodies (1 Cor. 3:16, 6:19,20).

Without the presence of God, **we are** but empty vessels.

"And at midnight a cry was heard: 'Behold, the bridegroom is coming; go out to meet him!"

- Matthew 25:6

The Shofar

The Trumpet

Traditionally the best man of the bridegroom would cry out, announcing the bridegroom's arrival, followed by the blowing of a **Shofar** (*ram's horn*). Most likely this would wake up everyone within hearing distance, and all would know by the sound of the blast that a bridegroom was coming for his bride. Some neighbors might even be so inclined as to come out and watch the festivities as the young men went charging into her home to kidnap, so to speak, her and her bridesmaids.

It might interest you to know that the earliest mention of a trumpet sounding was from God on Mount Sinai to announce His arrival to the people.

God told Moses-

> "...When the trumpet sounds long, they shall come

near the mountain."

-Exodus 19:13

When God announced His arrival, the tone of the trumpet was so long and ominous that the people trembled.

> "Then it came to pass on the third day, in the morning, that there were thunderings and lightnings, and a thick cloud on the mountain; and the sound of the trumpet was very loud, so that all the people who were in the camp trembled."

-Exodus 19:16

Of course, no one knows what kind of trumpet God used but we can all bet that it would have been magnificent to behold.

Over the centuries, there have been debates on whether or not the Torah was written in chronological order, specifically from Exodus to Deuteronomy. I only mention this because it would be hard for me to be accurate on which came first, the **Shofar** or the silver trumpets God instructed Moses to make.

With that said, I'm going to make an educated guess to the best of my knowledge, that is, that the silver trumpets came first. Otherwise, how did the Israelites get the idea of using a ram's horn as a communication tool?

In Numbers 10, God charged Moses with making two silver trumpets that were to be hammered out. These trumpets were to be used by the priests to call the congregation together, direct the movement of the camps, sound the alarm for battle, appointed feasts, and more.

It was important for the people to pay close attention to the sounds of the trumpet calls, for the message was in the sound blasts: the tone, the timbre, and the pitch transferred the information, and was used to communicate to the people what action was to be taken.

> "Even things without life, whether flute or harp, when they make a sound, unless they make a distinction in the sounds, how will it be known what is piped or played?
>
> For if the trumpet makes an uncertain sound, who will prepare for battle?"
> -1 Corinthians 14:7,8

The **Shofar** is mentioned in several other passages, and in fact, is very much used today. They are very popular among both Jew and non-Jewish cultures as a call to worship, Sabbath, and in bringing in the New Year, just to name a few. I would encourage you to do a study of the **Shofar** and its origin. I think you would be surprised at how extensive the study can be.

Today, there is only one **Shofar** sound, that all believers in Christ are in great anticipation to hear: the sound of our Bridegroom calling for His bride!

> "For the Lord Himself will descend from heaven with a shout, with the voice of an archangel, and **with the trumpet of God**, and the dead in Christ will rise

(*stand upright*) first.
Then we who are alive and remain shall be <u>caught up</u> (*raptured*) together with them in the clouds to <u>meet</u> (*encounter*) the Lord in the air. And thus, we shall always be with the Lord.

-1 Thessalonians 4:16,17

Also Paul writes-

> "Behold, I tell you a mystery: We shall not all sleep, but we shall all be changed-
>
> in a moment, in the twinkling of an eye, at the last trumpet. For the trumpet will sound, and the dead will be raised incorruptible, and we shall be changed."
>
> -1 Corinthians 15:51,52

In fact, did you know that there is a crown for those who anticipate the Lords coming?

> "Finally, there is laid up for me the crown of _____, which the Lord, the righteous Judge, will give to me on that Day, and not to me only but also to all who have loved His appearing."
>
> -2 Timothy 4:8

Made you look, didn't I?

Scripture References

The Bride of Christ

- John 3:30
- Acts 17:28
- Romans 12:1,2
- 1 Corinthians 2:9
- 2 Corinthians 5:5,17
- Philippians 1:21
- Colossians 1:9,10
- 1 Peter 2:9,10
- 1 John 4:9

The Shadchan

- Genesis 24
- John 3:16
- Ephesians 1:4
- Ephesians 2:4-6
- Ephesians 2:8
- Ephesians 2:16-18 (also used in The Ketubah)
- Ephesians 3:5,6
- 1 John 5:20

The Ketubah

- Matthew 13:45,46
- Matthew 20:28
- John 1:1,2
- John 10:10
- John 10:27-30
- John 14:20
- John 15:16, 19
- Romans 3:22-24
- Romans 5:8,9
- Romans 10:9-13
- Romans 8:15,16

Scripture References

- Romans 8:38,39
- 2 Corinthians 1:20
- Galatians 4:6
- Ephesians 1:5,6
- Ephesians 1:7
- Ephesians 2:13
- Ephesians 2: 16
- Philippians 2:8
- Philippians 4:19
- 1 Thessalonians 4;16,17
- 2 Timothy 3:16
- Titus 2:14
- Hebrews 12:2
- 1 Peter 1:18,19
- 2 Peter 1:3,4

The Sefel

- Deuteronomy 22:13-30
- Matthew 1:19
- Matthew 10:32
- Matthew 26:29
- Matthew 26:42
- Luke 22:15-20
- John 18:11
- John 19: 28-30
- John 19:28
- 1 Corinthians 3:16
- 1 Corinthians 6:19,20
- 1 Corinthians 11:25,26
- Galatians 3:13
- Ephesians 1:4
- Ephesians 1:7
- Ephesians 5:2
- Ephesians 2
- Ephesians 3:17-19

Scripture References

The Mattanah

- Genesis 24
- Numbers 36:7,8
- Matthew 6:25-34 (vs.32,33)
- Matthew 24:36
- John 14:1-3
- 2 Corinthians 1:20-22
- 2 Corinthians 5:5
- Ephesians 1:13-14
- Ephesians 4:7,8
- Ephesians 4:11,12
- Philippians 4:19
- Hebrew 13:5
- James 1:7

The Kallah

- Psalm 45:13-15
- Proverbs 13:20
- Matthew 24:42
- Matthew 28:1-13
- Matthew 28:19
- Mark 1:9-11
- John 13:34,35
- Romans 6:3,4
- Romans 10:9,10
- 1 Corinthians 6:19,20
- Galatians 2:20
- Galatians 3:26,27
- Galatians 6:9,10
- Ephesians 4:22-24
- Philippians 1:21
- Colossians 3:12-14
- 1 Peter 1:15,16
- Revelation 19:7,8

Scripture References

The Chupah

- Deuteronomy 22:8
- John 14:2,3

The Chatan

- Genesis 29
- Deuteronomy 22:13-21
- John 2:1-11
- John 3:29
- Acts 8:39
- 1 Corinthians 15:51,52
- 2 Corinthians 12:2-4
- 1 Thessalonians 4:15-17
- 1 Thessalonians 5:2
- 2 Peter 3:9,10,14,15

Scripture References

Appendix Chapters

A Nation is Born- Israel

- Genesis 12:1,2
- Genesis 13:11,14,15,17,18
- Genesis 15:2,3,4,5,6
- Geneses 16:1-4, 5-15
- Genesis 17:4-7, 15,16, 19,20
- Genesis 21:1
- Genesis 25
- Genesis 29:27,28
- Genesis 35
- Exodus 1:8,9, 10-14
- Exodus 12:40
- Exodus 19:5-8
- Exodus 24:8
- Numbers 23:19
- 1 Samuel 15:29
- 1 & 2 Kings
- 1 & 2 Chronicles
- Hosea 2:15,16
- 1 Thessalonians 5:24
- Hebrews 6:18

A Marriage Covenant of Laws – Broken More About the Shadchan

- Genesis 17:7
- Deuteronomy 7:3,4
- Deuteronomy 7:6-8
- Deuteronomy 24:1
- 1 Samuel 8:5-11
- 1 Samuel 8:18-20
- Isaiah 54:4-8
- Ezekiel 16 in its entirety

Scripture References
Appendix Chapters

More About our Shadchan

- Genesis 17:4
- Psalm 139:13,14
- Jeremiah 31:31-34
- Hosea 2:19,20
- Matthew7:
- John 1:12,13
- John 3:16,17
- John 10:28,29
- John 14:6
- Romans 8:14-17
- Romans 8:15
- Romans 8:23
- Galatians 4:4,7
- Galatians 3:26-29
- Ephesians 1:3
- Ephesians 1:4,5
- Ephesians 1:14
- Ephesians 2:8
- Ephesians 2:16-18
- Ephesians 3:5,6
- Colossians 1:15
- Colossians 2:9

More About the Cup

- Matthew 26:15,16
- Matthew 26:39,42,44
- Mark 14:23,24
- Luke 22:7,8
- Luke 22:14-16
- Luke 22:17-20
- John 1:29
- John 19:28-30
- 1 Corinthians11:23-25

Scripture References
Appendix Chapters

More About the Mikvah

- Exodus 19:10
- Exodus 30:17:24
- Leviticus 11
- Leviticus 14:8
- Leviticus 15
- Leviticus 16:17-24
- Leviticus 16:26-28
- Joel 2:32
- Matthew 3:11
- Matthew 10:32,33
- Matthew 28:18-20
- Mark 1:4,7,8
- Mark 16:15,16
- Luke 3:16
- John 11:55
- John 12:42,43
- Acts 2:38
- Romans 6:3,4
- Romans 10:9,10,13
- 1 Corinthians 6:11
- Galatians 3:26-28
- Ephesians 5:25,26

The Veil

- Genesis 17:4
- Genesis 24
- Exodus 25:22
- Exodus 25:31, 35-40
- Exodus 33:18-23
- Leviticus 10:3
- 1 Kings 8:1-11
- 2 Chronicles 5
- Isaiah 7:14

Scripture References
Appendix Chapters

- Matthew 1:21-23
- Matthew 27:50,51
- John 1:10,11
- 1 Corinthians 3:16
- 1 Corinthians 6:19,20
- Ephesians 2:8
- Ephesians 2:11-13
- Ephesians 2:14
- Ephesians 2:19
- Ephesians 2:21,22
- 1 Peter 2:4,5

The Shofar

- Exodus 19:13, 16
- Numbers 10
- Matthew 25:6
- 1 Corinthians 14:7,8
- 1 Corinthians 15:51,52
- 1 Thessalonians 4:16,17
- 2 Timothy 4:8

Reference Materials

Strong's Greek/Hebrew Definitions

Englishman's Concordance

Exegetical Dictionary of the New Testament

Louw and Nida Greek-English Lexicon of the New Testament

The Moody Bible Commentary (by Rydelnik & Vanlaningham)

Thayer's Greek Lexicon

Thayer's Greek Lexicon (Transliteral Greek)

Theological Dictionary of the New Testament

Vine's Expository Dictionary of New Testament Words

Word Meanings in the New Testament (by Ralph Earle)

Illustrated Manners and Customs of the Bible: by J.I. Packer, M.C. Tenney, Editors

Additional Information

A Christian Love Story: by Zola Levitts

In My Father's House: by Zola Levitts

Here Comes the Bride: by Richard Booker

Chuck Missler on the Rapture: Session One and Two- on YouTube

The Trumpet: The Shofar: Ancient Sounds of the Messiah by Richard Booker

The Kingdom, Power & Glory The Overcomer's Handbook by Chuck and Nancy Missler

About the Author

Caren Apple is a seasoned minister with over two decades of experience, known for her transformative work in spiritual growth. As the visionary founder of Acts of Faith Ministry and Bride of Christ Encounter, she has touched countless lives with her profound insights and unwavering dedication to faith.

For thirty-five years, Caren has walked hand in hand with her beloved husband, David, nurturing a partnership rooted in love and devotion. Together, they have raised two remarkable children, Mark and Bayleigh, who embody the values of compassion and service instilled by their parents.

Driven by an unyielding passion to illuminate the boundless love of the Father through His cherished Son, Jesus Christ, Caren exemplifies a life lived in purpose and devotion to spreading the message of faith and grace. Her commitment to empowering others on their spiritual journey serves as a beacon of hope and inspiration to all who are touched by her ministry.

Bride of Christ Encounter

If you would like more information about our Bride of Christ Encounters, women's ministry, please visit our website at www.bocencounter.org

We would like to extend a special invitation for you to come and experience this amazing time with us.

During these special Encounters, you will discover an ancient Jewish tradition of how a young man would go to such great lengths to pursue and win the heart of the woman he loves; whereby how this same tradition is followed precisely by Jesus, our Bridegroom, in a way that most of us haven't even realized.

With each Encounter, we will serve you brunch in a relaxing atmosphere surrounded by your fellow betrothed sisters. Afterward, there will be a 30-minute teaching as we will go over the 7 stages of betrothment followed by gifts bestowed upon you from your faithful Bridegroom.

On the last Encounter, you will take part in a Jewish

ceremony under a Chuppah with an extravagant reception to follow.

It is our hope, at the end of this Encounter, that you will know just how much God the Father has loved you from the beginning of time, how He strategically betrothed you as a bride to His beloved Son, and that by doing so, has made you His daughter, giving you the right to call Him "Abba Father."

Blessings,
Caren Apple

Contact Information for more about scheduling your own Encounter Retreat.

Tina Musto
Public Relations
bocencounter@gmail.com

www.ingramcontent.com/pod-product-compliance
Lightning Source LLC
Chambersburg PA
CBHW020930090426
42736CB00010B/1094